BAR
METR

BARCELONA
METROPOLITAN
Tales of Two Cities

Whit Stillman

Faber and Faber
BOSTON · LONDON

Barcelona copyright © 1992, 1994 by Film Barcelona, Inc.
Metropolitan copyright © 1988 by Whit Stillman;
copyright © 1989 by Westerly Film Video, Inc.
Introduction © 1994 by Graham Fuller

Excerpt from *How I Raised Myself from Failure to Success in Selling*
by Frank Bettger copyright © 1977, 1949 by Frank Bettger.
Reprinted by permission of the publisher, Prentice Hall/A division of
Simon & Schuster, Englewood Cliffs, NJ.

CIP records for this book are available from the British Library
and the Library of Congress
ISBN 0-571-17365-9

Printed in the United States of America

DEDICATION

This book is dedicated to the memory of the late
Brian Greenbaum, 1961-1992, the Brown University semiotics
school film production Rat Pack member whose brilliance,
charm and efficiency led to the realization of *Metropolitan*
and made *Barcelona* possible;

and to the late Ted Riley, 1918-1984, the philosopher-agent
whose wisdom, insight and humor enhanced the lives of his
family, friends, clients and even customers.

CONTENTS

Introduction by Graham Fuller   vii
Barcelona   1
Metropolitan   151

AUTHOR'S NOTE

The following scripts are not exact transcripts of the two films but the final shooting scripts for each. For the finished films a number of scenes were dropped or cut. Other scenes expanded, often with the restoration of material from prior drafts. With the advent of video, the publisher suggested that we leave that version as the transcript; here we show the original plan.

INTRODUCTION

Whit Stillman's Tales of Two Cities

As the red winds of *Killing Zoe, Natural Born Killers,* and *Pulp Fiction* blew through American theaters in the late summer and early fall of 1994, *Barcelona,* the second feature by independent writer-director Whit Stillman, offered a refreshingly tranquil breeze. It wasn't Stillman's subject matter—two callow young American men negotiating love and xenophobia in Spain—or his naturalistic style that made the movie so appealing. Rather, it was the urbanity of his storytelling, the lightness of his touch. There is no huff and puff in Stillman's work, no visible effort, though love and bombs go off and people experience watershed moments. If Stillman were a tennis player, we'd talk about his flicks of the wrist or his deft backhand lobs.

The son of an impoverished debutante from Philadelphia and a Democratic politician who went on to serve in the Kennedy administration, Stillman was born in 1952 and raised in Cornwall in upstate New York. He graduated from Harvard in 1973 and, having found a niche as a humorist on the college daily, started out as a journalist in Manhattan. Just before he married his Spanish wife in Barcelona in 1980, he was introduced to some film producers in Madrid and persuaded them that he could sell their films to Spanish-language television in America. As a result, he worked for the next few years as a sales agent for directors like Fernando Trueba and Fernando Colomo, also playing comic Americans in films like Trueba's *Sal Gorda.*

Stillman had already conceived the idea for *Barcelona,* but it was his script for *Metropolitan* (1990) that took shape first. He wrote it between 1984 and 1988 while running an illustration agency and admits now that its evolution was agonizing, a process of trial and error, although it would earn him an Oscar nomination for Best Original Screenplay. He financed the film from the proceeds of selling his apartment for $50,000 and contributions from friends and relatives that enabled him to complete it for $225,000. *Barcelona* would cost $3.2 million.

As a filmmaker, Stillman is a miniaturist with a restrained palette and a tone both genteel and droll. *Metropolitan* is a low-lit, low-key romantic comedy of manners about a group of New York preppies and the less affluent youth, Tom (Edward Clements), they befriend one Christmas, an incident inspired by Stillman's own experiences as a youth. Influenced by F. Scott Fitzgerald, the milieu of these young adults more closely approximates the work-free world of Jane Austen transplanted to hermetic haute bour-geois Manhattan. Its nominal heroine, Audrey (sensitively played by Carolyn Farina, appropriately en route to Scorsese's *The Age of Innocence*), is reminiscent of *Mansfield Park*'s passive maiden Fanny Price. In love with Tom, who likes but slights her in favor of an earlier love and gradually sees the error of his ways, Audrey is *Metropolitan*'s one untainted character. Her circle is made up of teenagers who occasionally seem snobbish or narcissistic or super-cilious. Yet, with the exception of the odious society rake, Von Sloneker, they resemble any other group of unformed young adults who think they know more than they do. Stillman's anthro-pological, fly-on-the-wall approach neither patronizes nor ridicules them. They may be children of privilege, but it doesn't follow that their feelings and opinions are contemptible.

Two of *Metropolitan*'s characters, the doleful, pontificating Charlie (Taylor Nichols) and the soigné, bitchy Nick (Christopher Eigeman), reemerge, for all intents and purposes, as *Barcelona*'s American cousins. Nichols plays the zealous sales director, Ted, a genuine eccentric who loves late-seventies disco music but pri-vately dances to Glenn Miller while studying the Bible; Eigeman is the truculent and somewhat feckless naval officer, Fred (actually an advance man for the Mediterranean-based Sixth Fleet), who has invited himself to stay at Ted's Barcelona apartment. The movie is set during the early eighties, when Spanish resentment ran high against NATO and America's self-appointed role as world policeman; its opening montage depicts attacks against U.S. targets in Barcelona. Fred, whose uniform marks him as a *"facha"* in the eyes of the locals and his behavior as a bloody-minded provocateur, quickly disrupts uptight Ted's diplomacy with his

Spanish friends and his quest to find a partner among the trade-fair girls he socializes with.

What makes the film succeed is the way Stillman draws the political into the personal, and vice versa, without relinquishing the wit or grace that characterized *Metropolitan*. In *Barcelona*, he sets up a dance-like confusion of sexual relationships—or temporary alliances. Despite Ted's avowed intent to date only homely women, he gets involved with the far-from-homely Montserrat (Tushka Bergen), and Fred with Marta (Mira Sorvino), both of whom are also sleeping with Ramon, a glib playboy journalist who has written a series of anti-American articles. When Montserrat lets slip at a party that Ramon sleeps around because he cannot perform with a woman he knows well, Fred seizes on the admission like a born sophist: "That's terrible! Poor guy. . . . But it explains a lot. . . . I think it's well know that anti-Americanism has its roots in sexual impotence. At least in Europe." This is the kind of delightfully fallacious reasoning that Nick used to vilify Von Sloneker's philandering in *Metropolitan*: in each film, the Christopher Eigeman character is playing a game of slippery Oedipal one-upmanship. Ted meanwhile seethes at Ramon's suggestion that the Americans themselves were responsible for the bombing of the USO building in which an American sailor has died. Ted is politically better informed than Fred, but his hostility is also personal: He wants Montserrat to leave Ramon and move in with him. Shortly afterward, during another political discussion at a country picnic with the Ramon set, Fred embarrasses Ted and alienates Montserrat and Marta by a symbolic act of hawkishness. In case we're in any doubt that Stillman is making Fred and Ted's sexual insecurities the "subtext" of their outraged nationalism, he playfully has them analyze that very word while they're walking to work one morning.

Stillman is a deft social ironist, and critics who assume that Ted and Fred are ideological ciphers or mouthpieces do so at their peril. We may grow to sympathize with Ted and Fred during *Barcelona*, especially when the latter is hospitalized by terrorists, but as American apologists they are as successful as Groucho Marx was a seducer. They are highly watchable characters, because of, not despite, their asperity. "Ted has a very high nerd-component for a motion picture leading man," Stillman has said.

If there is autobiographical content here, then there is also healthy self-satire. Even Ramon is not quite what he seems—and none of the women characters are, although the status of women in Stillman's work is complex. Marta in *Barcelona* moves from sweet plausibility to duplicity; she and the other women in the film are noticeably less quirky than Fred and Ted. Stillman does not depict women sentimentally, but rather as practical beings with strong survival instincts. There is the sense that the director is constantly reassessing his attitudes toward women and relationships between the sexes, and it's to his credit that *Barcelona*'s romantic resolutions are wholly unexpected.

For all of Ted and Fred's self-righteous indignation on behalf of America, they would never quote John Wayne like *Natural Born Killers*'s Mickey, whose murderous invocation to his partner-in-crime, Mallory—"Let's make some music, Colorado"—was affectionately lifted by Tarantino from *Rio Bravo*. But Stillman has his own kind of fun with a sacred-cow movie when intolerant Fred sneers at *The Graduate* for having Katharine Ross run off with "this obnoxious Dustin Hoffman character" instead of the "tall, blond, very popular" guy she has just married. In this way, Stillman offers a more oblique kind of perversity than a movie-fiend like Tarantino. Exactly because his innocents abroad—the needling Fred and his "Bible-dancing" cousin—are so unfashionably unhip, and so unlike any other characters you are likely to find in an American film in the 1990s, they are sublimely "cool." Their progenitor, meanwhile, is a rare and pleasingly literary voice in the increasingly inarticulate, blood-clotted world of popular cinema.

Graham Fuller, September 1994

Barcelona

Barcelona had its first public showing as the closing night film at the Seattle International Film Festival in June 1992. It opened theatrically in New York on July 29, 1994. The cast includes:

TED BOYNTON	Taylor Nichols
FRED BOYNTON	Chris Eigeman
MONTSERRAT RAVENTOS	Tushka Bergen
MARTA FERRER	Mira Sorvino
RAMON	Pep Munne
GRETA	Hellena Schmied
AURORA BOVAL	Nuria Badia
DICKIE TAYLOR	Thomas Gibson
THE CONSUL	Jack Gilpin

Cinematographer	John Thomas
Production Designer	Jose Maria Botines
Costume Designer	Edi Giguere
Editor	Christopher Tellefsen
Music	Mark Suozzo
Produced, Written and Directed by	Whit Stillman

Produced by Film Barcelona for Castle Rock Entertainment
A Fine Line Features release

EXT. PLAZA ADJ. AMERICAN LIBRARY — DAY

The American Library in Barcelona, early morning. All is peaceful.
A pedestrian crosses in front.

TITLE: Barcelona, Spain —
      The last decade of the Cold War . . .

Without warning a bomb blows up inside the building, blowing out
glass, doors and windows; clouds of dust and smoke billow out, flames
start up inside. As the smoke billows up and hangs in the air, a dissolve.
(Soundtrack: a woman's nearly suppressed sneeze overlaps the
dissolve.)

INT. BLUE APARTMENT — DAY

A puff of make-up powder raised by the sneeze of a young woman,
MARTA FERRER, *still only partly dressed, sitting at a desk trying to make*
herself up. She laughs. A tall man with longish hair, about ten years
older than she is, also only partly dressed, comes up behind her, takes
her face in his hands and turns it showing her profile in the mirror.

                    MAN
Perfecto.

After he moves away she continues looking at herself in the mirror a few
moments more.

EXT. STREET IN COMMERCIAL DISTRICT — DAY

The window of the IBM showroom on a Barcelona avenue. A rock or
brick is thrown through it, shattering the glass.

INT. BARCELONA TRADE FAIR — DAY

An aisle between company stands with industrial exhibits at Fira
Barcelona, the Barcelona Trade Fair. A well-dressed but otherwise
sympathetic-looking young businessman with a very serious, thoughtful
expression walks down the aisle. A beautiful young woman in a modish
outfit characteristic of an "azafata," one of the hostess-interpreters

3

working for the exhibitors at the fair, approaches from the other direction and smiles at him before they cross. TED BOYNTON, *not used to being smiled at, stops and watches her walk down the aisle criss-crossed by business-people and trade fair personnel.*

EXT. GOTHIC QUARTER — NIGHT

Tight shot of gargoyle waterspouts on the roofs of the old palaces spewing water during a rainstorm.

EXT. GOTHIC QUARTER STREET — NIGHT

In a dark street on a rainy night a cab lets off a naval officer in blue uniform. He crosses to a building doorway with his duffle bag and presses the intercom.

INT. STAIRWAY, SAME BUILDING — NIGHT

The stairway and foyer light, normally off, flicks on. Sound of someone coming down the stairs. Ted arrives at the bottom of the stairs and looks out at the shadowy form standing out in the rain.

> TED (*v.o.*)
> (*Peeved*) I couldn't believe Fred would just show up that way. On the other hand, it was absolutely typical.

Ted opens the door. FRED *bolts in out of the rain, shaking his cap and slicker off.*

> FRED
> Phew. Thanks.

Ted gingerly picks up Fred's wet duffle bag and leads him up the stairs. Whatever initial conversation they have is silent under Ted's voice-over.

> TED (*v.o.*)
> I was furious, but tried not to show it.

> TED
> (*Furious*) Jeezus – you could have called!

4

FRED

I did call. But it was one of those pay phones that cut you off and swallow the change.

TED

Oh: you called once from the airport.

FRED

At least once . . . I would not "not-call."

They climb the stairs in silence for a few moments.

TED

How, uh, long do you plan to stay?

FRED

That's a good question.

TED

You know what Dr. Johnson said . . .

FRED

No.

Ted pushes open the door and they enter his apartment.

TED

"Guests, like fish, begin to stink on the third day."

FRED

Actually, I think you'll find that I begin to stink on the first day. . . .

INT. CAFÉ — NIGHT

Fred and Ted with beer glasses at a table in the back of an uncrowded café as it fills up. Fred is immaculately dressed in his blue uniform.

TED

I saw the prettiest girl at the trade fair today.

FRED

You spoke with her?

Ted shakes his head "no."

5

FRED

Of course not.

TED

I'm beginning to reconsider my whole attitude toward female beauty. I think it's very bad, really. You see a beautiful girl and are immediately subject to all these emotions, some of them very powerful and almost uncontrollable.

FRED

Yeah, but —

TED

— They are. You haven't even spoken with a girl and already you want to marry and spend the rest of your life with her.

FRED

I —

TED

— This inordinate concern for physical beauty has wrecked more lives —

FRED

— Wrecked lives?

TED

Yeah, at the Lake, Charlie Johnson, uh —

FRED

— That was pathetic.

TED

There are so many cases. In our family, the whole Beautiful Boynton Sisters thing . . .

FRED

Is this related to you and Betty?

TED

No, that was different.

Ted looks away. . . . A group of young people, including three very attractive young women, enter the café. Ted looks at them and then

6

resumes his former position with a somber expression and takes a sip of his beer. Fred is still gawking at the girls.

EXT. STREET — NIGHT

Ted and Fred leave the café.

> FRED
> There were a lot of really attractive girls in that place.

> TED
> This is where the cool trade-fair girls come.

Fred takes out pen and notepad.

> FRED
> Great. (*Writing.*) "Cool trade-fair girls." That's terrific.

> TED
> Actually, a lot of people come here – it's quite popular.

Fred steps back to look at the name of the café and notes down the information.

> FRED
> I suppose if you wanted to meet cool trade-fair girls you could also go to the trade fair itself.

> TED
> Yeah, but the atmosphere's not so good – and the trade fairs are intermittent, while the girls come here all the time.

> FRED
> "Trade-fair girls off-season." Cool. Thanks. This is really good stuff.

> TED
> A lot of them studied in England and speak English with these terrific English accents.

> FRED
> That's good? I hate that.

> TED
> What?

A group of four young people pass them on the sidewalk.

> GIRL I

Facha.

> GUY I

Yanqui fora.

*Fred looks very surprised to be addressed in an apparently hostile way
by strangers in the street. He turns and looks at the group, which has
not broken its stride and is entering the café. The girl who called him
"facha" is wearing the uniform of jeans with a black leather jacket. The
whole group has a modish "tough" look, but not very tough.*

> FRED

Jeezus! What's that about?! . . . What does "facha" mean?

> TED

That's slang for "fascist."

> FRED

Fascist?!

Ted unlocks the car and they both get in.

> TED

Don't worry, they call everyone that. I mean, you comb your
hair, or wear a coat and tie, and you're "facha." A military
uniform – definitely "facha."

> FRED

So "facha" is something good, then. . . . Because if they were
referring to the political movement Benito Mussolini led, I'd
be really offended. Men wearing this uniform died ridding
Europe of Fascism.

INT. CATHEDRAL PLAZA – NIGHT

*Ted's car pulls to a stop in front of the cathedral's illuminated stained-
glass facade. Ted and Fred lean forward toward the front windshield to
get a better look at it.*

> TED

That's the cathedral.

                              FRED

Uhn-huhn.

Ted pulls the car forward another thirty yards.

                              TED

These are the remnants of the old Roman walls.

                              FRED

Uhn-huhn.

                              TED

(*Annoyed*) Listen, let's call it a night. You're obviously very
tired.

                              FRED

After what happened? I'm far too worked up to call it a night.
We had a very close call back there – it could have turned
really ugly. . . . They obviously didn't mean "facha" in the
positive sense.

*Ted has pulled the car back into the traffic heading for the center of
town.*

                              TED

With the whole controversy over Spain joining NATO, I'm not
sure this is a very good time for a fleet visit. There's a lot of
anti-NATO feeling here –

                              FRED

– Anti – What?!

                              TED

Anti-NATO.

                              FRED

Anti-*NATO?!*

                              TED

Well, here it's OTAN.

                              FRED

They're against OTAN?!

9

                              TED
Yeah.

Fred is still incredulous.

                              FRED
They know it's the *North Atlantic* Treaty Organization?
Canada, Norway, Denmark . . . Holland . . .

EXT. CAR ON AVENUE – NIGHT

*The car drives through the center of Barcelona, passing Plaza
Catalunya's illuminated fountains.*

INT. TED'S CAR – NIGHT

                              FRED
. . . If it were the *South* Atlantic Treaty Organization I could
understand their concern. . . . But this is the *North* Atlantic
Treaty Organization. It's been around for thirty years and
hasn't done anything. Actually it's quite pathetic –

                              TED
– What exactly are you doing here?

                              FRED
I'm sort of the advance man for the Sixth Fleet. . . . The last
fleet visit was a disaster. Their idea was to get someone in early
to smooth things out and make sure nothing goes wrong.

                              TED
That's going to be really tough. (*Pause.*) It's an assignment
that'll require a lot of diplomacy and tact. (*Pause.*) I'm really
surprised they gave it to you.

                              FRED
Well, it doesn't require that much tact.

                              TED
(*Nodding toward the window*) This is my favorite Barcelona
avenue – Paseo de Gracia. It's sort of the Michigan Avenue of
Barcelona.

FRED

Yeah, nice . . . You know, after all that's happened, I have a feeling I'm not going to be able to get to sleep tonight without something more to drink.

TED

The avenue up here's "Diagonal." . . . Actually, it's more like Michigan Avenue.

INT. BAR — NIGHT

In a well-lit and attractive bar of brass, glass and blond wood, Fred and Ted stand at the bar with small glasses of red wine.

TED

I've got a real romantic-illusion problem. This thing of always falling in love with incredibly attractive girls is – really bad.

FRED

What?

TED

I'm thinking of only going out with plain or even rather homely girls. . . .

Fred looks at him with surprise.

TED

I've got a real romantic-illusion problem.

FRED

Yeah.

EXT. TED'S CAR — NIGHT.

The car pulling incredibly slowly into the street.

INT. TED'S CAR — NIGHT

Ted and Fred back inside the moving car.

FRED

What if – and this is hypothetical – the one girl in the world

11

with whom you could be happiest – the girl with the most wonderful personality – or soul – imaginable – also happened to be incredibly attractive? According to your theory, you wouldn't even look at her.

TED

Oh, I'd look at her. I just wouldn't go out with her.

FRED

Your only chance for ultimate happiness would be gone.

TED

I guess it would be. (*Pause.*) I don't really buy that, that there's *just one girl who's right for you.* Things don't work that way. (*Pause.*) I'm sure there are a lot of terrific plain or homely women.

FRED

Okay. But what if you don't meet any of those terrific plain or homely girls? What if the only women you meet and like also happen to be incredibly attractive?

TED

Do you think I'm an idiot? Of course if the only women I meet that I like are attractive, I'd make an exception. (*Self-reproachfully.*) God, why did I tell you anything about this. I must be drunk . . .

FRED

No. You can confide in me.

TED

It was just an idea.

FRED

Well, good, because it sounded really pathetic. Crazy.

TED

Oh, thanks.

FRED

God, you're weird.

TED

Better weird than what you are.

EXT. TED'S CAR — NIGHT

Longer view of Ted's car.

EXT. ISOLATED STREET OUTSIDE CENTRAL DISTRICT — NIGHT

*Posters and anti-NATO, anti-American slogans fill one wall: "OTAN
– No! Bases fuera! Cerdos Yanquis Go Hoem!" (In a smaller grafitti
hand someone has added "en catala" — put it in Catalan.) Fred's
excited voice can be heard faintly from inside the slowly moving car:
"Stop the car, stop the car." It rolls to a stop along the curb opposite the
slogan-filled wall; Fred gets out and purposefully crosses the street,
where he stares at the insulting slogans. Ted steps up from the car
without leaving it, its motor and lights still on.*

FRED

"Cerdos." Pigs. They're calling us pigs. That's meant to hurt.

TED

Come on. Let's go.

FRED

Do you have paint or a marker of some kind?

TED

No. Come on. Forget it.

FRED

I'm not going to forget it. People have been forgetting things
far too long.

*Fred gets out his ballpoint pen and by making many strokes tries to form
a legible "Si" in place of the "OTAN-No." Ted walks across the street
toward him.*

TED

This is not our country.

Fred ignores Ted.

13

You shouldn't be doing that. We're guests here.

Fred first says nothing, then turns around and speaks to Ted with a surprising vehemence.

FRED

How blind can you be? . . . People like you make me sick.

Ted is taken aback by Fred's anger. A sedate young middle-aged couple walks down the other side of the street, watching them curiously. Ted, embarrassed, stands apart from Fred looking in another direction, as if he were uninvolved. Some sporadic traffic passes down the street. Ted turns back. Fred has added a "Si" to "OTAN" and is finishing putting an "X" over the "No."

TED

Okay. That's it. Let's go.

FRED

(*Turns around*) And just leave that – (*reading*) "Yankee Pigs Go Ho-em" . . .?

TED

Omigod! You're going to paint the whole wall with a ballpoint pen! Give me a break! I'm going.

Ted has turned to see whether anyone is observing them or about to pass by. He turns back to see Fred finishing interpolating an "i" between the "c" and "e" of "Cerdos" (pigs).

TED

Listen, I'm going.

Ted stands as if he is going to cross back to the car.

TED

I'm out of here.

Fred has put a short line through the "d" of "Cerdos," turning the letter into an ugly "b," and the word into "Cierbos."

TED

"Ciervo" is with a "v," not a "b."

14

FRED

Well, it's correct phonetically.

TED

(*Reading*) "Yankee Deers?" I don't see how it's much of an improvement. "Yankee Deers Go Home."

FRED

Would you prefer to be called a "yankee pig" or a "yankee deer"?

A car passing them suddenly brakes and comes to a quick stop twenty or thirty yards down the street. A young woman they cannot see calls to them from the car.

YOUNG WOMAN

Tayd!

The young woman gets out of the car and approaches Ted, smiling. Dressed as a fifteenth-century Spanish queen with a beautiful coiffure and opulent-looking dress, her identity is initially mystifying to him. Two other young women, dressed as the royal princesses "Las Meninas" from the Velazquez painting, look at them from the back window of the car. A Roman centurion is at the driver's seat. The queen is almost upon him before Ted realizes that she is MARTA FERRER *from the trade fair – the same young woman seen putting on makeup at the beginning of the film. Marta speaks English with a slight English accent but Spanish or Catalan intonations.*

MARTA

Tayd, what are you doing here? (*To Ted, after noticing Fred's uniform.*) You are going to the same party as we?

FRED

Yes.

MARTA

Good. (*Noticing grafitti.*) "Cierbos Yanquis?"

They all look at the wall. In the background the two princesses have gotten out of the car.

15

FRED

I don't think we've met. You're a royal personage of some kind?

MARTA

Queen Isabel.

TED

This is my cousin, Fred. (*To Fred.*) Marta works at the trade fair.

MARTA

(*To Fred:*) I like your costume.

Fred looks down at his uniform. The Roman legionnaire, in a toga and red feather-topped helmet, has meanwhile gotten out of the driver's seat and stands by his open door with an impatient look. A motorcycle carrying a couple in extravagant costumes passes them on the street.

MARTA

Have you no costume, Ted?

Two girls in costume on motorcycles, apparently friends of Marta's, stop near them.

CENTURION

(*Calling*) Vamanos!

MARTA

We must go.

FRED

Why don't we split up – I'll go in your car, and the princesses in Ted's?

MARTA

Yes.

Both look to Ted for his assent. Ted looks first at his watch and then at the princesses, who are quite homely.

TED

Okay.

They all head for the cars. Marta says something to the princesses so that they cross over to Ted's car. Fred takes a last look at his handiwork on the wall and then goes to get in the back seat of Marta's car.

INT. DISCO – NIGHT

Historical figures and others in fancy dress costumes dancing to disco music at nightclub such as UP&down. Fred, Marta and one of the plain princesses – AURORA – are at a small banquette table. In the background Ted is dancing in an imaginative way with the other plain princess.

                              FRED
He is not at all how he seems.

                             MARTA
No?

Fred shakes his head "no."

                              FRED
He might seem like a typical American – like a big unsophisticated child – but he's far more complex than that.

                             MARTA
Really?

Occasionally Marta and Aurora look in the direction of Ted on the dance floor.

                              FRED
Have you ever heard of the Marquis de Sade?

Both girls nod "yes."

                              FRED
Ted's a great admirer of de Sade, and a follower of Dr Johnson. He's a complex, in some ways dangerous man – he has a serious romantic-illusion problem. Women find him fascinating. (*Looks to dance floor.*) His nickname is "punta de diamante" – point of a diamond.

Both girls look in Ted's direction.

17

Do you see the odd expression on his face? Under the –
apparently very normal – clothes he's wearing are these narrow
leather straps, drawn taut so that while he dances . . . (*Fred
leans toward them and drops his voice, inaudible under the loud
disco music, with unintelligible hand language, before suddenly
stopping.*)

AURORA

What?

*Fred has noticed that Ted and the other princess have stopped dancing
and are coming back to the table.*

FRED

Please – don't mention this. He might feel I'd violated a
confidence.

Fred directs himself to Ted and the other princess.

FRED

(*Very friendly*) Hi.

AURORA & MARTA

Hi.

TED

(*Winded*) Whew. (*To other princess.*) Thanks very much.

AURORA

Sit here.

MARTA

Yes.

*Aurora and Marta eagerly make space for Ted to sit down between
them. They also allow some room for the other princess to sit. There is a
notable lull in the conversation.*

TED

What's wrong?

FRED

I was telling them your nicknames.

TED

(*Nervous*) You're kidding.

FRED

No, Marta wanted to know them.

MARTA

(*Smiling; still thinking it's something sexy*) Yes, Ted, what are your names?

TED

Don't get into that.

FRED

I only remember two others.

TED

Listen, don't get into that.

FRED

Oh, come on. What difference can it make now.

TED

Really. I mean it: DON'T.

FRED

Give me a break. I'm supposed to be the "childish" one.

AURORA

If he doesn't want to talk about it . . .

FRED

No, it's the principle of the thing.

TED

The principle!

FRED

(*Goes ahead regardless*) "Crusty Fusty" and "The Big 'O.'" Is that so bad?

TED

God. You jerk.

MARTA

What does that mean?

19

TED

I don't believe you.

Ted, tiredness suddenly catching up with him, gets up to go.

FRED

What's the big deal?

TED

It's just . . . lousy.

Ted says goodbye to the other princess and Aurora, who gets up, too; he's quite cool to Marta and glacial to Fred.

FRED

Oh, give me a break. Don't go.

TED

You were right – you do stink on the first day. (*To Marta and other princess.*) 'Bye.

Ted leaves, with Aurora walking with him as far as the exit. Fred and Marta watch him go.

FRED

(*After a pause*) That guy really gets to me. (*Pause.*) Okay – I tend to act like a jerk around him. But he provokes it.

MARTA

What do those names mean – they are related to his sado-masoquismo?

Fred, preoccupied, initially not paying attention.

FRED

No. . . . Something else. Did you hear that crack he made about my intelligence?

MARTA

No.

Fred keeps looking in the direction Ted left. Marta does too.

INT. MARTA'S APT./BEDROOM — DAY

At dawn in Marta's room Fred lies on the bed looking up at the ceiling, talking in a wistful, philosophical tone. Marta is with him. A sheet covers them, mostly.

FRED

Sometimes we think – well, we almost always assume we are going through life surrounded by people. Then something happens and you realize: we are entirely alone.

Tonight while I was shaving – I always shave against the direction of the beard, because I always understood you got a closer shave that way – I started thinking about this razor commercial on TV which shows all the hair follicles like this (*demonstrates with his fingers*), going this way; the first of the twin blades cuts them here, the hair snaps back and the second blade catches them down here – giving you a closer, cleaner, possibly smoother shave. That we know.

What struck me was that if the hair follicles are going this way, and the razor is, too – then they're shaving in the direction of the beard, not against it – which would mean that I've been shaving the wrong way all my life.

Maybe that's not so – maybe I've mis-remembered the ad. But the point is, I could have shaved the wrong way all my life and never known it. Then I could have taught my son to shave the wrong way, too, without him ever knowing it either.

MARTA

You have a son?

FRED

No, but I might some day. And then maybe I'll teach him to shave the wrong way.

While he talks Marta is looking more closely at the uniform tunic Fred has taken off.

MARTA

I think maybe my English is not so good. (*Pause; looking at uniform.*) Did you know that your costume has your name in it?

FRED

Let me see that. (*Looks.*) God, how odd.

Fade to black.

EXT. AVENUE — DAY

Spectacular girls on Vespino motorcycles converging from various directions, like horsemen coming together at a gallop in a Western. Some of the women are in trade-fair outfits.

INT. BLUE APARTMENT — DAY

A young woman in a trade-fair outfit, MONTSERRAT RAVENTOS, *hurriedly sits down at the same makeup-covered desk Marta used before. While reaching for her makeup, she notices something out of place and the thin coating of powder spread over the desk. She touches it, leaving a mark in the dust. Somewhat disconcerted and preoccupied, she looks in the mirror to put on her makeup when the same partially dressed tall man,* RAMON, *comes up behind her, takes her face in his hands and turns it, showing her profile in the mirror.*

RAMON

Perfecto.

MONTSERRAT

(*Very skeptical*) Perfecto?

RAMON

Casi perfecto. (*Almost perfect.*)

MONTSERRAT

(*Now somewhat disappointed*) Casi?

INT. BEDROOM, BLUE APARTMENT — DAY

Montserrat, fully dressed and made up, enters the bedroom to take off the bedclothes. She strips off the top sheet and separates it from the blanket, takes off the bottom sheet and the pillowcases.

INT. HALLWAY & BATHROOM, BLUE APARTMENT — DAY

Montserrat walks briskly down the hall carrying the white sheets, enters the bathroom and gets ready to stuff them in the laundry hamper when she notices something. Balancing the laundry on the top of the hamper, she peels off two very long hairs. She examines them closely, comparing them to her own.

EXT. FIRA BARCELONA — DAY

Panorama of the Barcelona Trade Fair's spectacular campus, with a trade show in full swing. The camera tracks and pans down to street level, where trade-fair girls on motorcycles and others are arriving and heading for the exposition halls.

INT. EXPOSITION HALL, FIRA — DAY

Montserrat, looking depressed and somewhat preoccupied, walks down the central corridor carrying a clipboard and folder of papers. She steps up to the IHSMOCO stand, greeting NURIA *and leaving some papers with her before moving on. Ted, standing in the back of the stand talking on the phone, idly watches Montserrat's approach while finishing the call and hanging up. As Montserrat walks down the corridor, Ted distractedly looks after her a moment before looking the other way. Coming the other way, Aurora Boval, one of the plain "princesses" from the previous evening, catches his eye and smiles.*

> AURORA

Hola, Tayd!

> TED

Hola.

> TED *(v.o.)*

Fred's thesis that maybe I'd never meet any of the terrific plain girls was already inoperative. Aurora Boval had invited me to a Lionel Hampton concert she had tickets for Thursday night.

EXT. OFFICE BUILDING, U.S. CONSULATE – DAY

Fred, in uniform, walking by two Spanish policemen carrying submachine guns at the entrance of the office building housing the U.S. Consulate.

(*Insert:* OFFICIAL SEAL OF THE U.S. CONSULATE)

TED *(v.o.)*
Meanwhile, Fred felt that the start of his work was less than a complete success. . . .

INT. CONSULATE OFFICE – DAY

Fred sitting in a consular office. A foreign service officer faces him, holding a sheaf of telexes, an incredulous expression on his face. The Consul puts his hand on his forehead and through his hair.

FRED
I saw it more as a judgment call.

CONSUL
You were unaware of this order?

FRED
Well, I thought that just applied to the, uh, khaki uniform. I didn't realize it meant the blue one, too.

CONSUL
(*Pause*) You're ROTC, aren't you?

FRED
Yes, I am. (*Pause.*) This order—I must admit, I'm a little troubled by it. Men wearing this uniform died freeing Europe from Fascism. I'm proud of this uniform. It seems a bit cowardly –

He notices the consul's expression and stops.

FRED
The thing is, I don't have any good civilian clothes. . . .

24

INT. TED'S APARTMENT — NIGHT

Ted has just gotten back from work (8:30 or 9 p.m. in Spain) and is shedding his suit jacket and opening a beer bottle, with conversation in progress.

> TED
>
> . . . really well. We introduced a high-speed motor suitable for use in the new generation of "smart" textile machinery. How was yours?

> FRED *(o.s.)*
>
> Frankly . . . not so great.

Show Fred, totally demoralized and slumped in an armchair, dressed in a hideous combination of clashing civilian clothes: madras jacket, bermuda shorts, an orange novelty shirt, disgusting slippers, tiger-striped socks.

> FRED
>
> Do you think you could lend me some clothes?

INT. TED'S ROOM — NIGHT

Fred and Ted examining clothes in Ted's closet.

> FRED
>
> The blue one, I think.

Ted takes out the hanger with a blue suit on it and gives it to Fred, who starts trying the jacket on.

> FRED
>
> You really don't mind my borrowing it?

> TED
>
> (*Extremely long pause*) No.

> FRED
>
> Really?

TED

It's, uh, okay.

INT. BATHROOM AT TED'S APT. — NIGHT

Fred at mirror shaving. Ted, finishing his beer, speaks from the bathroom doorway, which is adjacent to the kitchen. Music, a sixties-style soul song, plays from Ted's stereo in the living room. The conversation is in progress.

TED

Spanish girls tend to be really promiscuous.

FRED

You're such a prig.

TED

I'm not using "promiscuous" pejoratively. It's just a fact – they have a completely different attitude toward sex.

FRED

You're such a prig.

Ted disappears as if offended. Fred glances to where Ted was before vanishing as if maybe regretting having gone too far. Then Ted reappears with a bottle of beer.

TED

Okay, I'm a prig. But now I'm speaking sociologically. The sexual revolution hit Spain later than the U.S. but went far beyond it. I'm not sure how it was in other cities and towns but in Barcelona, everything was swept aside. . . . The world was turned upside down, and stayed there.

FRED

Has it ever occurred to you that maybe the world was upside down before, and is now right side up?

He looks at Ted in the mirror.

TED

No, I don't think that's it.

Ted turns and leaves, a bit low.

26

INT. LIVING ROOM — NIGHT

Ted sits on the sofa reading a large gilt-edged book hidden inside a copy of The Economist *magazine. Fred looks in the mirror, tying his tie.*

TED

... I'm doing something with Aurora tomorrow so I thought I'd just do some reading tonight.

FRED

Aurora?

TED

The very nice, rather plain girl with Marta last night. She had extra tickets for a jazz concert at the Palau.

FRED

Phew, a jazz concert. That's tough. You really are polite . . .

INT. APARTMENT FOYER — NIGHT

Ted is at the door to see off Fred and Marta, who are about to go out. While Fred is wearing the blue suit, Marta is grimly dressed in a black leather jacket and black chinos.

FRED

This is the way you dress to go . . . OUT?

MARTA

Yes.

TED

Your trade-fair outfit's so cool.

MARTA

(*Groans*) Uh! Those clothes are *awful*.

TED

Really? I think they're cool.

Fred finishes straightening his tie in the mirror.

FRED

I don't get it: I always look so much better in mirrors than photographs . . .

27

(To Ted:)

Sure you don't want to come?

TED

No.

FRED

Good.

Marta kisses Ted on both cheeks.

MARTA

Adeu.

TED

Adeu.

FRED

Bye.

Ted waits a moment as they head down the stairs, then closes the door.

TED (v.o.)

Except for work I had been in a serious funk for some time. I would never mention something like that to Fred. He was the last person to trust with a personal confidence of any kind.

Montage under Ted's voiceover: Ted in kitchen, opening refrigerator and preparing tray.

Carrying a tray with a beer and plate of crackers and cheese to the table. Turning on his stereo's radio tuner to the local golden oldies station, which occasionally plays real oldies (Glenn Miller, etc.). At the table, Ted picks up his copy of The Economist *and removes the large black book hidden inside it. It has* The Holy Bible *in gilt letters on the cover and yellow Post-it notes all over and inside it. He opens the book with one hand and with the other pours his beer.*

I don't know whether I had found God since coming to Barcelona or was just going through a religious phase. It had all begun shortly after the incredibly sad and guilt-ridden breakup with Betty . . .

BETTY'S APT., CHICAGO – NIGHT *(Visual-only flashback)*

Soundless scene of Ted breaking up with BETTY – *a pretty young woman in attractive, sedate clothes – her features contorted with unhappiness and broken-hearted pain; she's crying and talking a blue streak, recriminations directed at Ted, interrupted by sobs and emotional collapse. It is a harrowing scene; the "dark underside" of failed romance.*

. . . with whom I had gotten deeply involved, including carnally, despite never having really loved her. The almost irresistible attraction of physical beauty had transformed a good friendship into another horrible premarital situation. All this had led pretty directly to the Old Testament.

The Glenn Miller classic, "Pennsylvania 6-5000," comes on and Ted perceptibly sways to it while still reading scripture.

TED *(v.o.)*
Two Old Testament books in particular – *(Inserts of titles: "Ecclesiastes" and "Proverbs.")* – included advice on romantic matters, some of it very tough.

Ted standing up and plausibly dancing or moving in tune with the Glenn Miller song while still reading scripture.

After what happened with Betty I had resolved not to sleep with any girl until I met the one I wanted to marry and spend the rest of my life with. I had no idea if I'd ever meet such a person or if she even existed, plain or not. My aspiration was to free romance from the chains of physical beauty and carnality – and to stop doing harm.

A shot of a thoughtful, dancing Ted from a new angle reveals Marta and Fred standing at the opening to the living room silently watching him Bible-dance. After a moment Ted notices them or Fred breaks the spell.

FRED
What's going on?

TED
What are you doing here?

FRED

What is this . . . ? Some strange Glenn Miller-based religious
ceremony?

TED

No. Presbyterian.

FRED

Good. . . . Listen, I didn't have time to change any money
today.

TED

How much do you need to change?

FRED

Would a hundred dollars be possible . . .?

*When Marta follows, it becomes apparent her presence makes Ted
nervous, so she sits down on the sofa. Fred follows Ted to where he has
his secret stash.*

FRED

(*In a quiet voice*) I don't actually have the dollars on me now,
I'm waiting for a transfer through American Express.

TED

You want to borrow ten thousand pesetas? Just say so.

*Ted going through the rigmarole of getting the money out from where it's
hidden, maybe not very anxious for Fred to see exactly how he gets it
out and how much it is, either – the stash includes several thousand
dollars of Spanish and other European currencies for Ted's business
travels.*

FRED

I could give you a chit for it.

TED

What I'd like is the money back.

FRED

Of course.

Ted, looking skeptical, carefully rehides his stash.

INT. FRONT DOOR, TED'S APARTMENT — NIGHT

Marta has already started down the stairs. Fred, just leaving, turns back to Ted.

>   FRED
> You'll get it back.

>   TED
> Sure.

Fred, very annoyed at Ted's skepticism, gives him a hard look and starts down the stairs. Ted turns into the apartment, swinging the door shut after him.

Fade to black.

EXT. PASEO DE GRACIA — DAY

Long shot of Ted walking up Paseo de Gracia on his way to his office.

>   TED *(v.o.)*
> What made my isolation in Barcelona bearable was work for IHSMOCO.

INT. OFFICE BUILDING — DAY

Ted opening the door of the IHSMOCO office.

>   TED *(v.o.)*
> Like nearly everyone else . . .

MONTAGE — CULTURE OF SALES

A montage of images illustrating Ted's "culture of sales" voice-over—Private boys' high-school production of what might or might not be Death of a Salesman; *Prof. Thompson's class in college; IHSMOCO's sales department at the start of the flu epidemic; the covers of classic books in the literature of sales—winding into the café scene further below.*

31

TED *(v.o.)*

. . . I had seen Arthur Miller's play and as a youth had the usual sneering, deprecating attitude to the world of business and sales. All that changed senior year, when the charismatic professor Woodward Thompson's business course convinced us that even the apparently mundane world of business had its romance. A job interview with IHSMOCO led to employment in its training program. We were supposed to rotate between departments but I arrived in sales just as the flu epidemic struck, and never left. In sales I found not just a job but a culture. Franklin, Emerson, Carnegie and Bettger were our philosophers, and thanks to the genius of Carnegie's theory of human relations, the so-called Dale Carnegie system, many customers also became friends.

INT. CAFÉ – DAY

Ted in animated conversation with Catalan businessman friend standing up at a café.

TED

I don't consider high-pressure sales sales at all. It's a form of fraud. In true sales you're providing a real and constructive service – helping people make their lives more agreeable, or their companies more efficient, and in so doing creating wonderful economies of scale from which everyone and the whole economy benefit.

BUSINESS FRIEND

You are right, Tayd. That is so.

TED

I mean, look around – (*Indicates beautiful street outside with all its hubbub.*) – all this, everything we see, was built with sales.

Ted and the businessman look around, impressed.

TED *(v.o.)*

The classic literature of self-improvement – unlike some more recent bestsellers – really was improving.

INT. OFFICE — DAY

During a lunch break Ted eating a sandwich at his desk and reading Frank Bettger's classic, How I Raised Myself from Failure to Success in Sales. *Nuria eats a salad at her desk while perusing a copy of* Marie Claire.

TED

(*To Nuria:*) Here's something really good:

Nuria looks up with interest.

TED

It's Bettger quoting George Matthew Adams: (*Reading.*) "The wisest and best salesman is always the one who bluntly tells the truth about his article. . . . That is always impressive. And if he does not sell the first time, he leaves a trail of trust behind . . . being bluntly honest is always safe and best."

INT. TED'S KITCHEN — NIGHT

TED *(v. o.)*

Other books, magazines, and audiotapes mixed practical tips with home truths.

Ted at home working standing up at the kitchen table strewn with papers and an adding machine. A time-management audiotape plays on his stereo.

AUDIOTAPE *(o. s.)*

Try this: each time you handle a paper on your desk, mark it with a red dot. If you later encounter papers with three or four dots, you could be working more efficiently. Try to dispose of each piece of paper the first time you handle it.

Ted leans down, picks up a red pencil and marks each paper with a red dot.

INT. TED'S APARTMENT — DAY

Early one morning, Ted is getting ready for work, with Fred, out of uniform, hanging around in annoying mode.

33

TED *(v.o.)*

The enthusiastic, unsophisticated tone of much of this
literature did open it up to the facile ridicule of half-wits.

FRED

Maybe I could use the same self-motivational techniques you
use in sales in my navy career:
  "Every day in every way I'm becoming a better and better
lieutenant junior grade. Every day in every way I'm becoming
a – "

TED

– What you're referring to is "autosuggestion," popularized by
Coué during the twenties but totally unserious. What I'm
talking about has nothing to do with that.

INT. TED'S OFFICE – DAY

*Return to Ted as he was at the beginning of montage, entering his
office. He turns on the lights and walks toward his desk when the telex
machine jumps into noisy operation, attracting him to it. Close shots of
the telex terminal in operation form a loving but fast montage of a now
anachronistic technology.*

TED *(v.o.)*

I loved coming into the office early and catching up on the
overnight telex traffic. The telex line was our umbilical cord to
Chicago, and confirmations for the bigger sales came through
it too.

Simultaneously Ted reads the new message as it prints out:

TO: ALL REGIONAL DIRECTORS

EFFECTIVE JUNE 24 RICHARD TAYLOR OF
MARKETING WILL ALSO BE SUPERVISING SALES.
ALL REGIONAL DIRECTORS SHOULD REPORT TO
HIM.

SINCERELY

HENRY FERRIS – VP SALES

Ted, looking stunned, rips off the telex sheet and reads it again, walking back to his desk. He slumps down in his desk chair, the kind that has wheels. A key can be heard in the office door lock. Nuria opens the door and comes in.

NURIA

What is wrong?

TED

Dickie Taylor's going to be supervising sales.

NURIA

The Deekiee Taylor of Marketing?

Ted nods his head "yes."

TED

I can't believe it. Work for that guy? (*Very somber.*) I'm sure he's going to get me fired.

NURIA

No. You are the best they have. They cannot do that.

Ted, very depressed, makes an expression of skepticism.

EXT. PALAU DE LA MUSICA — NIGHT

That night Ted waiting outside the "Palau," Barcelona's art nouveau concert hall. Many attractive people, including women, pass by Ted as they enter for the jazz concert.

Montage: Aurora – the camera looks into her eyes.

TED (*v.o.*)

I'd really looked forward to seeing Aurora that night. I had this image stuck in my mind of looking into her eyes and maybe seeing her soul. But she was late, which was actually not that common in Barcelona.

Ted stares around. In the background a poster announces that night's concert artist as "Vinyl Hampton—the latest in progressive jazz from Canada" (in Catalan).

MONTSERRAT

Oh, it's you.

Ted looks at her, puzzled.

MONTSERRAT

Aurora can't come. Please excuse my retard.

Montserrat gives Ted his ticket.

INT. PALAU DE LA MUSICA CATALANA – NIGHT

Montserrat talking very quickly to Ted as they sit in their seats before the concert. Conversation in progress.

MONTSERRAT

Two weeks ago Aurora had a flechazo – (*she indicates hands grasping an arrow in the heart*) – and –

TED

– What's a – (*makes similar gesture*) – "flechazo"?

MONTSERRAT

It means suddenly dropping crazily in love with someone – as if an arrow had entered your heart, shot by one of those little-boy angels. Aurora had a crazy adventure with this very handsome man. But he got too serious. She was about to begin an adventure with you –

TED

– An "adventure"?

Montserrat shakes her head "yes" and continues.

MONTSERRAT

– But her boyfriend got angry and pressured her.

TED

Aurora has a boyfriend?

MONTSERRAT

Yes.

Ted, surprised and pensive, turns and looks down at the simple jazz concert program with, in large letters, the name of the performer – "Vinyl Hampton."

> TED
> (*Looking at program*) I was sure Aurora said *Lionel* Hampton would be playing tonight. I never heard of *Vinyl* Hampton.

EXT. PALAU – NIGHT

Ted and Montserrat leaving the Palau as the concert ends.

> TED
> How could you tell I felt that way?

> MONTSERRAT
> During the whole concert your expression was like this:

She makes a face imitating Ted with the intensest frown possible. It's a bit exaggerated.

> TED
> You're very perceptive.

Montserrat laughs.

> MONTSERRAT
> What?

> TED
> You're very perceptive.

> MONTSERRAT
> What?

This time Ted repeats the words very slowly, pointing to her to indicate "you" and pointing to his eyes to indicate "perceptive":

> TED
> You-Are-Very-Perceptive.

> MONTSERRAT
> – Oh – Thank you.

TED

I don't really like perceptiveness of that kind.

INT. CHAMPAGNE BAR — NIGHT

Ted and Montserrat sit at a table along the wall.

TED

It's a typical pretty-girl thing – using observation for ridicule, as if impertinence were cute and charming. . . . My impression is that someone like Aurora would be more apt to use observation for comprehension, not –

MONTSERRAT

(*Surprised*) – You don't think Aurora is pretty?

TED

No . . .

MONTSERRAT

But she's beautiful. . . .

TED

Physically?

MONTSERRAT

Yes, her eyes . . .

TED

You think she's beautiful because of her eyes?

MONTSERRAT

Yes. She also has a beautiful . . . figure. . . .

TED

She does?

MONTSERRAT

Oh yes. (*Pause.*) Apparently, you are just the sort of "dangerous" foreign man she likes.

TED

What do you mean?

MONTSERRAT

(*Laughs*) Your brother told her about your . . . interests.

TED

What?

MONTSERRAT

You know . . .

TED

No.

MONTSERRAT

The Marquis de Sade . . . games of leather, weekends of fun. . . . The straps under your clothes –

TED

– He said that?

Montserrat nods "yes."

TED

That's completely untrue – I can't believe it. (*Pause.*) He promised he wouldn't say that anymore. (*Pause; then emphatically.*) He's *not* my brother.

MONTSERRAT

You don't know anything about the Marquis de Sade at all?

TED

No.

MONTSERRAT

Well – I don't believe you.

INT. DISCO – NIGHT

Montserrat and Ted walking away from the quite wild lounge area of a very popular disco. Ted is buttoning his shirt and tucking in his shirttails.

MONTSERRAT

So you're not wearing them tonight. That doesn't prove anything. . . . Maybe they're at the cleaners.

INT. DISCO DANCE FLOOR — NIGHT

Montserrat and Ted dancing superbly together on semicrowded dance floor.

> TED *(v.o.)*
> It turned out that we both loved the disco music of the late 1970s, despite what everyone else thought.

INT. DISCO BANQUETTE TABLES — NIGHT

Ted and Montserrat seated, in intense conversation.

> TED *(v.o.)*
> We talked about all kinds of things.

> TED
> You know how at parties people always talk about marketing?

> MONTSERRAT
> No.

Ted gives her a look of surprise and amazement.

> MONTSERRAT
> I've never heard people at a party talk about marketing.

> TED
> *(An incredulous pause, then continues)* Well, this idea of marketing being a science – if you look at the evidence, it's all anecdotal.

INT. DISCO DANCE FLOOR — NIGHT

The dance floor with Montserrat at center, smiling a lot. (If Ted is shown, he is, despite everything, a cool dancer.)

> TED *(v.o.)*
> I think it was during a Donna Summer song that it really happened, or at least that I realized it had.

EXT. BARCELONA STREETS – NIGHT

Ted walking home along the darkened city streets with the orange-uniformed cleaning brigade and guards the only people out.

> TED *(v.o.)*
> Everything was completely different now.

INT. TED'S APARTMENT – DAY/DAWN

*Fred is dressed, reading a newspaper (*El Periodico*) when Ted comes in.*

> FRED
> *(Reading, not looking up)* The things they say about us – I know you're not supposed to take it seriously – but after a while . . . it really hurts . . .

> TED
> *(Furious)* I don't believe you!

Fred looks up.

> TED
> Just once I'd like to go out with a girl not convinced I'm encased in black leather underwear!

> FRED
> That bothers you?

> TED
> The exact same story, over and over again!

> FRED
> Well, it's not exactly the same. I always vary it a little.

> TED
> Oh, great! It wasn't even Aurora but this terrific friend of hers from the trade fair. She's never met you but was still full of your stupid stories.

FRED

Frankly, I don't care for your tone. You should get down on your knees and thank God you have a cousin who makes up interesting stories about you. I'm the best P.R. guy you'll ever have – Do you think any even mildly cool trade-fair girl would give you the time of day if she knew the pathetic, Bible-dancing goody-goody you really are?

Ted turns around and wordlessly heads out of the room. Fred speaks louder as Ted goes farther away.

You're far weirder than someone merely "into S&M." I mean they have some kind of tradition, we have some idea what S&M is all about –

Ted's door can be heard slamming off screen.

(*Raising his voice further*) – there're books and movies about it. There is nothing to explain the way you are.

Fade to black.

EXT. MARTA'S NEIGHBORHOOD – TWILIGHT

First a long shot of Fred and Ted walking rapidly up hilly street of a residential neighborhood in upper Barcelona just below Travesera de Dalt, then a closer traveling shot. They say nothing to each other as they walk. Ted is particularly cold in his manner.

Fred sees something and stops.

FRED

Look.

From where they stand they can observe the patio behind Marta's apartment, where Marta, Montserrat and two other young women in casual clothes are practicing dancing "Sevillanas" with music from a small record player. For a while they watch in silence until Montserrat sees them.

MONTSERRAT

(*Smiling*) Hi, Tayd! Go to the front and we will come down.

42

Marta waves too and they both go inside the apartment. Fred and Ted start walking around to the front of the building.

INT. TAPAS BAR — NIGHT

Montserrat, Marta and Fred standing up having red wine and tapas at a cool Barcelona bar – either an atmospheric old place or a designer new one.

> FRED
>
> Haven't you noticed the way he's always making little digs about my intelligence?

> MONTSERRAT
>
> No.

> FRED
>
> You see, in the U.S. we take these tests called "college boards" to see whether the university we go to is "selective," "highly selective," or "not-at-all selective" – which is where I went. My "board scores" were very bad.

> MARTA
>
> But you seem very intelligent for an American.

> FRED
>
> Well – I'm not. (*Still somewhat incredulous.*) But the worst was Ted getting all-800 boards – perfect scores. Since then, though, I've met other people with 800-boards and they don't seem particularly smart, either.

Ted reappears at the other end of the room, returning from the pay phone or men's room, and walks toward them.

> MONTSERRAT
>
> So Ted is very smart. (*Looking in his direction.*)

> FRED
>
> Well . . . he tests well.

INT. ANOTHER BAR, RESTAURANT OR DISCO – NIGHT

Fred, Marta, Montserrat and Ted sit talking at a table. Marta is lighting a cigarette.

MARTA

I think it's true that the height of the sexual revolution is over. I don't go to bed with just anyone anymore. I have to be attracted to them sexually.

TED

But . . . I always thought that women had to have some profound emotional bond with a man, a secure romantic relationship, before they became interested in a . . . relation . . . of that kind.

MARTA

No.

Montserrat and Fred also shake their heads "no."

INT. TED'S BEDROOM – NIGHT

Light from street lamps and traffic filters into the room. When Montserrat speaks, Ted watches her with a look of utter devotion.

TED

Taking advantage of his position to get involved with a fifteen-year-old student . . . !

MONTSERRAT

Actually nothing happened until summer, by which I had sixteen years.

TED

(*Sardonically*) Oh, well – sixteen!

MONTSERRAT

Also, I had something to do with it.

TED

Still. Just from the little you've said, I really hate that guy.

MONTSERRAT
In truth, much of what you say reminds me of Ramon then.

Ted looks surprised.

MONTSERRAT
Ramon soon left from teaching to return to the newspaper. He had read the works of Philip Agee and so was an expert on the American CIA and its involvement in the internal affairs of every country. He would write a series of articles which were also destined to become a book.

Then, one year, the correspondent of fashion of his newspaper fell ill before the collections of Milan and Ramon was sent in her place. Before, Ramon had been always indignant about the terrible waste that high fashion represents. It was one of the things for which he most respected the East Bloc: there were not the wasteful, constantly changing fashions.

TED
Oh, terrific.

MONTSERRAT
Ramon came back from Milan with a new idea, which he conceived as the idea of physical beauty.

TED
What's that?

MONTSERRAT
His thought was that beauty is the closest thing to divinity that remains in the modern world. "All the Old Gods Are Dead" – there is no God, that we know – but in beauty the memory of divinity remains. Beauty is the memory of the ideal.

TED
(*Really interested*) Hunh.

MONTSERRAT
For always afterwards "Beauty" was the subject Ramon wanted to dedicate his journalism to.

TED
He wanted to write about flowers and things?

45

MONTSERRAT

No, it was the beauty of the female face and form that fascinated Ramon.

TED

Oh.

MONTSERRAT

Ramon transferred to the "style of life" section of the newspaper where he did serieses on photographers' models and on the young women who aspire to be actresses. Then he became interested in the beautiful women who remain, unknown, in the private world. He compared them to the flowers in the forest which no one ever sees. He did series on the most beautiful women of Barcelona and each of the surrounding cities and towns – Santa Coloma, Sabadell, Prat de Llobregat . . . Then he did series on the most beautiful school students of each town. The articles were accompanied by photographs and, as Ramon is a good writer, were very popular with readers.

TED

That makes sense. There's something very powerful about the idea of physical beauty. He's not stupid.

MONTSERRAT

It was important for Ramon's career as a journalist. He started appearing on television and to spend part of each month in Madrid. But our physical relation ended almost for completely. He wanted an open relation and encouraged me to link with other men.

TED

What?

MONTSERRAT

He thought I should link with other men.

TED

But you refused.

MONTSERRAT

No.

A long pause while Ted tries to take this in, or tries not to.

TED

When did you break up?

MONTSERRAT

(*Doesn't understand*) Break UP?

She indicates an up movement questioningly.

TED

Separate, break apart as a couple.

MONTSERRAT

No, we have not broken apart.

Ted looks disbelieving.

MONTSERRAT

We live together.

A long pause.

TED

So this is just some . . . "flechazo"?

MONTSERRAT

This?

Fade to black.

INT./EXT. TED'S APARTMENT — DARK DAWN/DAY

Ted's apartment still in the semidarkness before anyone's gotten up. The sound of a terrible explosion not far away. Fred and Ted rush out of their rooms.

FRED

Jeezus, what was that?!

They rush out to the balcony to take a look down the street, over which hangs a huge cloud of smoke.

                              FRED
       That's where the USO is!

EXT. STREET — DAWN HALF-LIGHT/DAY

Ted and Fred run two blocks down the street toward the smoke and are among the first to arrive at the scene of destruction. The doors, windows and interior of the USO center have been blasted away or entirely transformed. On the street a bloodied woman passerby is sobbing, leaning next to a car with someone helping her.

INT. USO CENTER — DAY

Inside is a ghastly scene of blood and mayhem. A sailor with blood all over his face and uniform kneels over the body of another sailor, who lies on the floor partially dismembered, writhing in death agony. The uninjured sailor, FRANK ROBINSON, *is trying to stanch the flow of blood from his comrade's body with a roll of plastic Saran Wrap.*

                             FRANK
       Hank. Hank. Stay with me, man. Stay with me.

In the room are five other people, the breakfast crowd at the USO that morning, all injured to some degree. Boxes of Rice Krispies, Corn Flakes, and chocolate-flavored Cocoa Puffs and their contents are strewn around. There's a severely dented cannister of Maxwell House coffee.

Fred yanks a stretch of electrical cord from a lamp or appliance. Kneeling alongside Frank he uses it to try to tie a tourniquet around the wounded sailor's dismembered arm to stanch the flow of blood.

                              FRED
       Jeezus.

                             FRANK
       Hang on. We'll get you home.

                               48

Ted has meanwhile rushed out to the street, as the sounds of an ambulance's horns approach in the distance. Ted reappears.

TED

The ambulance's coming!

The injured sailor has given up any visible signs of life. Fred stops.

FRED

He's dead.

TED

You can't be sure.

Fred puts his hand on Frank's back.

FRED

I'm afraid your friend's dead.

TED

We've got to get him to the hospital. Where's that ambulance? I'm sure there's some chance.

EXT. STREET OUTSIDE USO — DAY

A final shot of Montserrat and Marta in the crowd of onlookers, who watch the body being brought out, the blood and general mayhem with appalled expressions.

EXT. AIRPORT — NIGHT

Lights and movement in the desolate working area of the airport.

TED *(v.o.)*

That night Fred thought we should wait with the sailor from Brooklyn for the midnight plane that was going to take his friend's casket back home.

INT. AIRPORT HANGAR/CARGO AREA — NIGHT

Fred and Frank in uniform with black armbands, Ted in a dark suit and VICTOR — *a tall, hip-looking Barcelonan with a trumpet case — sit*

49

around the dead sailor's flag-draped casket in a desolate cargo hangar. Frank's face is covered with red marks from the bomb blast, and two Band-Aids.

> FRANK
>
> He had a good voice – very deep. He liked to sing those old Johnny Cash songs.

> FRED
>
> I really like those – "Ring of Fire."

> TED
>
> Yeah.

> FRANK
>
> He hoped to be sort of the Brooklyn Johnny Cash.

> TED
>
> God. . . . What a shame. . . . That could have been really cool. . . .

> VICTOR
>
> Yohnny Cash?

> FRANK
>
> Yeah.

Victor and Ted nod. Outside a cargo plane can be heard approaching the hangar. Fred has taken an old half-full bottle of Old Crow bourbon whiskey out of a bag and started pouring shots into plastic cups.

> TED
>
> (*To Fred, indicating the bottle*) Where'd you get that?

> FRED
>
> Uh . . . the Consul.

> TED
>
> So, he's not such a bad guy.

Fred distributes the glasses.

> FRED
>
> Well. . . . We'd better get started.

They get to their feet holding their shot glasses.

INT. HANGAR PASSAGEWAY — NIGHT

The camera follows a cargo vehicle moving at top indoor speed down a passageway leading to the hangar. In the distance the others can be seen improvising a service next to the casket.

> FRED *(almost o.s. in distance)*
> (*Reading from notes*) "Preserve us from the dangers of the seas, and the violence of enemies; bless the United States, watch over all that are upon the deep, and protect the inhabitants of the land in peace and quiet."

The cargo vehicle comes to a stop.

> FRED
> "All hands bury the dead.
> "Unto Almighty God we commend the soul of our brother departed . . ."

Fred nods to Victor, who gets out his trumpet and starts playing "taps." Fred, Ted, Frank and the cargo worker carry the casket to the wagon of the cargo truck, which drives away while the taps continue. Frank is quite broken up.

Slow fade to black.

Fade up:
TITLE: The Night of San Juan

EXT./INT. TED'S CAR — TWILIGHT

Ted and Montserrat in Ted's car driving past an intersection where a group of youths is building a bonfire of discarded furniture. Fire-crackers, cherry bombs and homemade rockets of various kinds are starting to go off.

> MONTSERRAT
> There are very many parties tonight – at least three we should go to.

                         TED
Three parties?

                    MONTSERRAT
Or four.

                         TED
Will that guy be at any of them?

                    MONTSERRAT
(*Nods*) I'm sure.

EXT. TOWNHOUSE PARTY — TWILIGHT/NIGHT

*In the front patio of an old townhouse like the restaurant Dos Torres an
early-evening party is beginning. When Ted and Montserrat arrive,
Fred is on the fringe of the party, as if about to go for a walk. Montserrat stops to talk with a group on the side. Fred – who is again
wearing his uniform, but now with a black armband – immediately
approaches Ted.*

                        FRED
Wow, this is bad. People are really unfriendly.

                         TED
I can't believe you're wearing that uniform. Are you out of
your mind?

                        FRED
This is the correct uniform.

                         TED
You're supposed to be acting diplomatically here.

                        FRED
I can't help it. I'm a sharp dresser. Blue favors me.

                         TED
I thought you already had this out with the Consul; he said it
was an order.

                        FRED
Well, I've thought more about that, and I think it was more a
guideline.

                          52

TED

Where's Marta?

FRED

(*Looking off*) I don't know.

Montserrat disengages herself from the person she was talking to and starts in to the party, toward Ted, who starts in, too. Fred walks a few steps with Ted, confiding in a hushed voice:

FRED

Listen, I'm only speaking English here. I don't want them to know how good my Spanish is.

INT. ELSEWHERE, PARTY — TWILIGHT/NIGHT

Montserrat and Ted inside the townhouse (or the garden in the back), looking toward the other side, where Ramon is dominating a conversational grouping. A strikingly pretty young woman sits by his side.

TED

That guy's here.

MONTSERRAT

Yes.

TED

Do you want to go?

Montserrat shakes her head "no."

INT. RAMON'S NOOK, PARTY — NIGHT

Group including Marta listens to Ramon very intently. A snatch of what Ramon's saying is just barely audible in passing.

RAMON

. . . Representantes del poderoso sindicato norteamericano, el (*in English*) "AFL-CIA," vinieron a Europa . . .

Through the rest of the sequence Ramon and his group can periodically be seen in the background.

53

INT. ELSEWHERE, PARTY – NIGHT

Fred with two young women who look like they might work at the trade fair, though now they're dressed in the grim, dark "party" clothes of the period – black leather jackets, etc.

FRED

"Trigger-happy"?! I don't see where you get that. The armed forces of the United States haven't fired a shot in anger in over . . . twelve months. We haven't even fired a shot in mild disapproval.

WOMAN I

You cannot say Americans are not more violent than other people.

FRED

No.

WOMAN I

All those people killed in shootings in America?

FRED

Oh, shootings. Yes, but that doesn't mean Americans are more violent than other people. We're just better shots.

INT. NEARBY, PARTY – NIGHT

Montserrat listening intently while Ted talks.

TED

. . . By the mid-fifties, when Jack Tyrrell took over, IHSMOCO was on the verge of insolvency. The truth is that Illinois High-Speed Motor's motors were no longer very fast. Jack re-focused IHSMOCO on what he saw as its real business: "This means motors and they must be fast," he would say. . . . Jack's one of those magnetic personalities from the World War II generation – he was with Wild Bill Donovan in the OSS and parachuted into Sicily before the Allied landings; his stories are amazing. He's supposed to come to Barcelona this summer; I hope you'll get a chance to meet him.

MONTSERRAT

Why is it that you think I should meet him?

TED

Because he's the last of the greats.

MONTSERRAT

It must be wonderful having a work you like and a boss you admire so.

TED

Yeah, it is. . . . Actually, lately there've been some problems. I don't know what's going on. I haven't heard from Jack in ages and he's put this terrible guy from marketing in over us – Dickie Taylor –

MONTSERRAT

– Deeckiee Taylor? –

TED

He's this incredible jerk who *Fortune* magazine included in their cover story on the – (*a derisory snort*) – "new generation of marketing geniuses" – as if marketing people weren't conceited enough.

Fred approaches, looking somewhat shaken.

FRED

Jeezus . . .

TED

What's wrong?

FRED

The anti-Americanism here is virulent.

TED

What were they saying?

FRED

I don't even want to get into it.

TED

It was that bad.

FRED

Yeah, I think so. I couldn't really follow it all.

Fred notices the bad jazz music.

FRED

This music – I don't get it – how could anyone dance to this?

One of the women Fred was talking with before – Woman 2 – rejoins them.

MONTSERRAT

It's not dance music.

FRED

(*With heavy irony*) Well, that explains it.

TED

(*Dislikes it too*) What is it? It sounds familiar.

WOMAN 2

Eet's Vinyl Hampton.

TED

Oh, God.

FRED

(*Heading for stereo*) Isn't there any dancing at parties here?

Fred moves to where the stereo and records are nearby. Woman 2 goes with him.

WOMAN 2

It's too early for dancing.

Fred looks at his watch.

FRED

No.

WOMAN 2

You don't like jazz?

FRED

No.

Fred meanwhile looks intently through the records.

56

WOMAN 2

I've never heard of anyone who didn't like jazz.

FRED

Really? How odd.

WOMAN 2

You really hate jazz?

FRED

(*Turns to her*) My jazz rule is: If you can't dance to it, you don't want to know about it.

WOMAN 2

I'm very surprised that an American does not appreciate jazz.

FRED

Well, you know, surprise can be good. (*Finding old record.*) Fabulous – this's great. Let's try it.

WOMAN 2

It is jazz?

INT. ELSEWHERE, PARTY – NIGHT

Ted and Montserrat talking.

TED

I just have the feeling the eighties are going to be a great decade.

MONTSERRAT

I also.

Suddenly the music blasts out a well-known Caribbean limbo song from the sixties – perhaps "Limbo Rock" with its catchphrase "How Low Can You Go?" Both turn to see Fred approaching them with a stick of some kind. Fred ropes the couple sitting next to them into holding what passes for the limbo stick. Fred, Montserrat and Ted try to get the dancing going. Others at the party begin to stare and Fred calls them to join in.

FRED

(*Enthusiastically*) Ahora, todos!

57

Fred leads Montserrat and Ted in going under the limbo stick. Aurora Boval arrives from another part of the house, full of enthusiasm to join the dancing.

AURORA

Hola, Tayd!

TED

Hola.

Only the four actually dance. Of the others, only Aurora's boyfriend and one of the other trade-fair girls seem even friendly bystanders.

FRED

(*While dancing, to the couple*) Un poco mas bajo?

He indicates "a little lower" with his hand. Marta, subdued, appears and watches them critically. Almost everyone else remains where they were sitting or standing, watching the dancing with some embarrassment. With the stick lowered the limbo dance doesn't really go so well. While Montserrat tries, Ted and Fred exchange words.

TED

(*Winded*) You know, this is almost impossible to do.

FRED

(*Winded*) I always forget that.
 Maybe it is too early.

As the "limbo" heads for fiasco, a view of everyone watching them. The expressions are grim.

INT. RESTAURANT "FLASH FLASH" — NIGHT

Montserrat, Fred and Ted at a table at a bustling, informal but modish late-night restaurant.

TED

Take hamburgers. Here "hamburgesas" are really bad; it's known Americans like hamburgers – so again – we're idiots. They have no idea how delicious hamburgers can be, and it's this ideal burger of memory we crave, not the disgusting burgers you get abroad.

FRED

We can't even call ourselves "Americans." They love to correct you, saying "South Americans are 'Americans' too." Give me a break.

MONTSERRAT

"Norteamericano" is the correct term.

FRED

But that makes no distinction between us and Canadians. (*A pause for emphasis.*) "Yanqui" and "Gringo" are obviously pejorative. But it's the standard dictionary term that's most insulting of all – "Estadouni-*dense* – *dense* – d-e-n-s-e: dense, thick, stupid. Every time you hear it – (*pantomimes someone being slapped on each "dense"*) Estadouni-dense, dense, dense – it's a direct slap in the face. I mean, it's incredible.

MONTSERRAT

I think you're too sensitive.

FRED

Oh, great, now we're too sensitive.

EXT. STREET OUTSIDE "FLASH" – NIGHT

The dark and narrow street outside "Flash" is deserted. From various parts of the city fireworks and firecrackers sound. The door to the restaurant abruptly swings open and Fred stalks out and down the street. Ted comes out after him.

TED

Fred!

Fred continues walking at a steady pace; Ted runs to catch up with him.

TED

Listen, I'm sorry. . . . Are you joking? . . . Fred?

Fred stops and turns around.

TED

You weren't really offended by that, were you?

FRED

No, I like being called dishonest.

TED

I didn't call you dishonest.

FRED

I'm not a thief.

TED

Well, you could be a lot more careful.

FRED

When we were kids I borrowed some things. It was never ever theft. In each case I either told you, or was about to.

TED

I was just joking. You're really overreacting.

Fred says nothing for a few moments but just stands absolutely still, thinking, calming down.

FRED

(*Now very calm*) You're right. I somewhat overreacted. Before I realized it I was out the door and it would have been really embarrassing just going back and sitting down again. (*A puzzled look.*) There's something strange about the coffee here.

TED

In Barcelona?

Fred nods "yes."

FRED

I think it's really messed me up. . . . And you're so con-descending. You think I went into the navy because I was too dumb for finance or something, that I washed out at Shearson.

TED

I have no idea what happened in New York.

FRED

I didn't wash out. There was no disgrace. They said I could go back. . . . I hated the idea of being stuck indoors for the next forty-five years, with two weeks off to go snorkeling annually.

A naval officer has one of the only white-collar jobs where you really deal with the physical world all day long and it counts, it's not theoretical. You dominate all four dimensions without a slipup or it gets very wet.

Montserrat has come out of the restaurant. She is curious and slightly perplexed.

Then there's all the fighting-for-freedom, defending-democracy, shining-city-on-a-hill stuff, which as you know I really buy.

TED

Jeezus. That's right. You do.

One of the uniformed waiters has come out of the restaurant, apparently concerned that they might be skipping out on their bill.

MONTSERRAT

The food has come.

INT. RESTAURANT "FLASH" — NIGHT

The three are finishing their meal. Leaning over talking with them from another banquette table is a suited young American executive.

TED

This is the way I see it: Work is better in the U.S. Living is better in Barcelona. The question is, what's more important – life or work? (*A suspenseful pause.*) Obviously – work.

AMERICAN EXEC.

Obviously.

FRED

(*Still chewing*) Oh, obviously.

The waiter delivers the check. Fred has gotten out his notepad and pen.

FRED

(*Mouth full*) I think I'll mention this place in *Port Call*.

He picks up the check and examines it.

But expensive.

61

Fred quickly passes the check to Ted, who takes out his wallet to pay it. Fred leans back to address the American executive.

                              FRED
    Have you been over the trade fair yet?

                         AMERICAN EXEC.
    No. I want to go.

                              FRED
    It's terrific.

EXT. STREET — NIGHT

Montserrat, Ted and Fred walking away from the restaurant. The fireworks frenzy of the night has finally erupted in the normally quiet area.

                              FRED
    It must have been like this the night Francis Scott Key wrote
    "The Star-Spangled Banner."

                              TED
    Yeah.

From the other direction, visible only in silhouette, a lone young woman walks irregularly toward them. Then she stops. It's Marta.

                             MARTA
    You've already finished?

                              TED
    Yeah, it's like two a.m.

                             MARTA
    Ramon was talking so fascinatingly I stayed to listen him.

                              FRED
    What was so, uh, fascinating?

INT./EXT. TED'S CAR — NIGHT

The four drive through the L'Eixample or Gracia districts, dodging amateur fireworks and still-smoldering bonfires set earlier. Possible

*montage: a father supervising his young son setting off terrifying rockets;
real fireworks on the skyline over the city; puffs of smoke and explosions
of the amateur variety everywhere. Ted drives with Montserrat next to
him; Marta sits in the back but leans forward; Fred leans back,
occasionally looking out the window.*

MARTA

. . . He described how after World War II representatives of
the American labor union, the AFL-CIA, were sent to Europe
to crush progressive unionism.

TED

How did they do that?

MARTA

With sacks of money and the anti-Communist tactics of your
Senator Jzo-ay McCarthy.

FRED

The AFL-CIA?

MARTA

(*Increasingly exasperated*) America's largest union, terribly
right-wing and facha – you have not heard of it?

Fred leans back as if he's afraid she's going to explode in his face.

MARTA

It's amazing the things Americans don't know about their own
country.
   Parece mentira.

A kid's rocket hits their car or cherry bomb explodes next to it.

EXT. PLAZA, GRACIA – NIGHT

*The Plaza del Sol in Gracia full of grim-looking young people – on one
side a banner proclaims the third European Jazz Festival. Marta and
Fred, walking in single file and not talking, cross briefly quite far ahead
of Montserrat and Ted, who walk together and are talking.*

TED

There's no such thing as the "AFL-CIA." It's the AFL-CIO –

63

actually AF *of* L-CIO – it was formed when the American
Federation of Labor merged with the more militant CIO.

> MONTSERRAT

How do you know so much about it?

> TED

Chicago's probably the capital of twentieth-century American
trade unionism. And the American labor leaders who came to
Europe then – Jay Lovestone and, uhmm . . . – were giants.

> MONTSERRAT

So what Marta said was partly true.

> TED

What do you mean "partly true"? I mean – they were people.

> MONTSERRAT

I'm sure I've heard of the AFL-CIA. There is some important
American labor union of that name.

INT. NEW PARTY – NIGHT

*It might be a garden or a spacious interior. At the other side a young
man sitting with a group of friends plays Bob Dylan or Dylanesque
songs on an acoustic guitar.*

> TED

There's an empty room where you could work during the day.

> MONTSERRAT

(*Smiles*) Are you proposing we shake up together?

> TED

"Shack up together." You use the expression "shacked up"
when you don't like one of the people involved. You and
Ramon were "shacked up together." We'd just be living
together.

> MONTSERRAT

What about Fred?

> TED

He's moving out.

Ramon and his coterie arrive at the party. Ramon is still accompanied by a beautiful young woman, INGRID, *who looks like she could be a Swedish model or something.*

> TED

God.

Ted half looks away.

> MONTSERRAT

She's a model he was interviewing.

> TED

He's just all work. What a creep.

> MONTSERRAT

(*Pause; thoughtful*) Ramon might not be as bad as you think he is.

Ted looks very skeptical.

> MONTSERRAT

There is a reason he goes with so many women. (*A pause; somewhat reluctant.*) Ramon has a problem. . . .

> TED

What?

> MONTSERRAT

After he knows a woman well, he cannot have sex with her well.

> TED

He has a sexual impotence problem of some kind?

> MONTSERRAT

Yes. Of some kind.

Fred rejoins them, having eavesdropped from nearby.

> FRED

That's terrible! Poor guy. . . . But it explains a lot.

> TED

What?

FRED

I think it's well known that anti-Americanism has its roots in sexual impotence. At least in Europe.

MONTSERRAT

What?

FRED

You haven't heard that? . . . This is not a put-down. I love Europeans. Amo los Europeos. Me encantan. But the link between European anti-Americanism and problems of a sexual nature was, I thought, well established. (*To Ted.*) Where was that research done? Suffolk University in Great Britain?

MONTSERRAT

To explain European anti-Americanism you need look no further than the U.S. itself.

FRED

Oow – ouch.

TED

(*To Montserrat:*) That's a widely held view. But if you look closer, you'll find it's not true.

FRED

Please don't misunderstand – I sympathize with your friend's problem. I once experienced something similar. It's terrible. (*Real sympathy.*) You see some anti-American tirade on TV, or in the newspaper, and you think: Poor guys. It's sad that just when there's so much interest in sex and so much of it so readily available, there should also be so much impotence . . . so much anti-Americanism . . . (*To Ted.*) There's no union called the AFL-CIA, is there?

TED

No.

FRED

I mean, give me a break.

INT. LATER, PARTY — NIGHT

There is now some good dance music and it's late enough for others to join in. Four or five couples dance in all – Ted with Montserrat, and Fred with an unknown woman. As usual, Ted's dancing is quite impressive.

INT. ELSEWHERE, PARTY — NIGHT

Within Ramon's smaller coterie, his Swedish girlfriend is speaking in English.

> INGRID
> . . . but an American sailor died in the bombing. I find it hard to believe even the Americans would kill their own people.

From some distance away, Ted, with Montserrat, listens with mounting anger.

> RAMON
> No. There is actually a long history of bloody American "provocations" of this kind. This bombing reminds one strongly of the United States' blowing up its own ship, the *Maine*, in Havana harbor as the pretext for starting the War of 1898.

> INGRID
> But, for what, a pretext?

> RAMON
> The American elections are approaching. A quick attack on some foreign "bogeyman" – Libya or Iran – might rescue the American president's reclining popularity. The American Sixth Fleet, which was to have "shown the pendant" in Barcelona this week, is still sailing the South Mediterranean awaiting such a pretext.

> INGRID
> Americans seem like big, oafish children – until you realize the evil they do.

67

RAMON

Even for me, who am cynical about these things, it is difficult
to believe.

INT. NEARBY, PARTY — NIGHT

*Ted, enraged, and Montserrat, nervous, still listening to Ramon from
some distance away when Fred shows up with drinks for Montserrat
and himself.*

TED

(*To Fred:*) Did you hear that?

FRED

Yeah. Poor guy.

TED

— The most disgusting slanders you can imagine! Someone's
got to say something.

FRED

No — don't.

TED

This — this — this scumbag is going around saying that the USO
bombing was "arranged by the Americans themselves." (*To
Ramon.*) That's a lie!

RAMON

(*Cool and amused*) What?

TED

(*Uncool*) Everything you've said.

RAMON

The Americans' exploding of their own ship, the *Maine,* in
1898 is an historical fact established well. The other is still a
thesis, but an increasingly likely one.

TED

Both are disgusting lies.

Everyone nearby is watching, with Ted unfavorably viewed.

> MONTSERRAT
> No, Ted, all the history books say that –

Ted gives her a look of betrayal.

> MONTSERRAT
> – about the *Maine.*

Ramon turns back to his group, very obviously cutting Ted.

> TED
> That's fine with me . . . (*turning*) . . . scumbag.

Ted walks away in a trancelike rage.

INT. ELSEWHERE, PARTY – NIGHT

Fred catches up with Ted. Montserrat is some ways off.

> FRED
> Jesus, Ted, I'm the one who's supposed to go berserk.

> TED
> You could've helped me out back there.

> FRED
> I can't get in political arguments. And you, uh, did fine.

> TED
> Oh, yeah. I made a complete fool out of myself. It's one of the
> first rules of sales – *never* get involved in matters of public
> controversy. But I couldn't *not* reply.

> FRED
> No . . .
> Don't get in a funk about it. Who was really listening – four
> or five drugged-up good-timers at some party? –

> TED
> – Twenty people at least. –

FRED

– Okay. You made a fool of yourself in front of twenty or thirty people. So what.

Fade to black.

EXT. THE SIXTH FLEET AT SEA — TWILIGHT/DAY

The Sixth Fleet cruising somewhere in the Mediterranean in the very late afternoon twilight.

TITLE: Somewhere in the South Mediterranean.

INT. TED'S APARTMENT — TWILIGHT/NIGHT

Ted and Fred after work drinking beers. Conversation in progress.

FRED

No, I really like it here. I'm really comfortable.

TED

It's just that we talked about your staying three days. It's already been much longer. With the fleet delayed, I thought you'd want another place to stay.

FRED

No. (*Looking around.*) This is nice.

TED

The thing is, I'm trying to get Montserrat to move in.

FRED

Well, that's great. I really like Montserrat.

TED

Weren't you thinking of staying at Marta's?

FRED

No. (*Pause.*) Since being here I've begun to realize how important family is. You and I are family. I want to be with family now.

TED

Yeah, well I want to be with Montserrat.

FRED

(*Turning a little petulant*) I'm really surprised at you – shacking up with her. I thought that would be against your morals or something.

For a while Fred tries to ignore Ted, looking elsewhere, then gives up.

FRED

You really want me out of here, don't you?

Ted nods his head.

EXT. COUNTRY ROAD – DAY

Ted's car driving down a country road in the rich agricultural Ampurdan region, northeast of Barcelona.

INT. TED'S CAR – DAY

Ted is driving with Montserrat in the front passenger seat; Marta and Fred sit in the back. Some picnic accoutrements are in view. Fred stares out his window in a somber mood. Some of Ted's and Montserrat's initial dialog is over a closeup of Fred looking out the window.

MONTSERRAT

. . . I still need to pick up my music from his apartment.

TED

What music?

MONTSERRAT

My radio (*ra-dee-oh*) cassette and tapes of music.

TED

The situation is still pretty raw. You really need those things urgently?

MONTSERRAT

I really need them urgently.

71

TED

It just seems unwise to go back so soon after you broke apart.

FRED

(*Looking out window – a loud snort.*)

TED

(*Looking back in the mirror*) What's that mean?

Fred's response is delayed. After a moment he looks forward blankly and turns again to look out the side window.

FRED

(*Almost inaudibly*) Suit yourself.

Fred continues looking out the side window. The three others all look somewhat disconcerted by his alienated weirdness.

EXT. MEDIEVAL HAMLET IN COUNTRYSIDE – DAY

Ted driving his car carefully through the narrow walled streets of a tiny hamlet, finally pulling into a grassy area by a large stone house where several other cars are already parked. They all get out and carry baskets into the old house, except Fred, who stays aloof and continues to act oddly.

INT. PASSAGEWAY, HOUSE – DAY

Ramon is horsing around with an attractive dark-haired young Spanish woman in front of a mirror in the old house. They are whispering and giggling or the Ramon equivalent. The others arrive and walk through the passage, out toward the garden, maintaining the civilities, exchanging "holas," with Ramon kissing the girls on the cheek. Ted tries to exchange a pained look with Fred but gets no response.

Ramon stops Montserrat, "Montse," and speaks with her briefly while Ted and Marta walk on ahead; Fred lags somewhat behind. Once they are out of Ramon's earshot, Ted questions Marta.

TED

(*To Marta:*) Who's the girl?

MARTA

She's an actress.

TED

What a creep.

EXT. GARDEN — DAY

In a shady patch of garden eleven picnickers sit on the grass on cushions from the garden furniture or low-slung garden chairs. The food is set up nearby on a table on the covered interior garden court. Fred is still sullen. JORGEN, *a Danish man about forty-two with thinning blond hair, speaks angrily.*

JORGEN

What it's about is a big country – the United States – making war on a little country!

TED

In the U.S. Government's view – which I am not in any way endorsing –

Fred, sitting apart and looking down, snorts at Ted's pusillanimity.

– the U.S. policy is – Well, let me put it this way . . . Maybe an analogy would help. (*Pointing to the grass.*) Take these ants.

Ted indicates a community of black ants in the soil nearby.

In the U.S. view a small group – or cadre – of fierce red ants have taken power and are oppressing the black-ant majority. The stated U.S. policy is to aid those black ants opposing the red ants in the hope of restoring democracy, and to impede the red ants from assisting their red ant comrades in neighboring ant colonies –

RAMON

– That is the clearest and most disgusting description of U.S. policy I have ever heard! The Third World is just a lot of ants to you!

JORGEN

(*Really upset*) Those are people dying, not ants!

73

TED

No, you don't understand. I was reducing everything to ant scale, the U.S. included – an ant White House, **an ant CIA,** an ant Congress, **an ant Pentagon.**

RAMON

(*Seething with contempt*) Secret ant landing strips, illegally established on foreign soil.

Abruptly Fred comes out of his sullen trance.

FRED

Where are the red ants?

TED

There.

Ted points out a small patch of soil in the grass where there are some red ants. Fred raises his arm with a rock in his hand and slams it down on top of them. Looks of shock and consternation cross the faces of everyone there except Montserrat, who, preoccupied with her own thoughts, wasn't really looking. Ramon looks at Fred with particular loathing.

EXT. HAMLET GRASSY AREA WITH PARKED CARS – DAY

Fred and Ted alone some distance from the house. Ted is furious.

TED

That was really terrible.

FRED

You're blowing it way out of proportion.

Ted just keeps shaking his head in consternation.

FRED

Don't take it so seriously. Those red ants were bad news. They weren't any good for anybody.

In the background Montserrat has come out of the house and started to walk toward them, her expression ambiguous.

TED

I was trying to convince them to think of Americans in a new

74

way. Then in one stupid move you confirm their worst
assumptions.

FRED

I did not confirm their worst assumptions. I *am* their worst
assumption.

Montserrat reaches them.

MONTSERRAT

(*To Fred:*) Now Ramon is certain you're CIA.

TED

(*Still seething, imitating Fred*) "Where are the red ants?" Whunk!

FRED

It was a joke. I'm not going to apologize. Those little bastards
got what they deserved.

EXT. GRASSY AREA, ELSEWHERE — DAY

*Some distance away, in the beautiful late afternoon light, a poignant
encounter between Montserrat and Ted seen from afar, with a disagree-
ment of some kind and Ted getting quite overwrought. He turns and
leaves and they walk away in opposite directions, Montserrat rejoining
a group of people by the house that includes Ramon and his date. Ted
arrives back at the car in a black mood and gets in, saying nothing to
Fred, who leans against the other side. Marta approaches and Fred
opens the front passenger door for her. Instead, without looking at or
greeting him, she gets in the back seat.*

FRED

Oh, thanks.

*Fred, beginning to get fazed by everyone's hostility, gets in the front
passenger seat himself.*

INT. TED'S APARTMENT — NIGHT

*Fred's bags and personal effects are in an orderly pile near the door. Ted
goes around straightening up and arranging things in the apartment.
He looks at the clock, which says 2:30.*

From the little balcony overlooking the street Ted checks to see if anyone – such as Montserrat – might be coming, but the street is deserted.

A reflective Ted, wearing pyjamas, sitting on his bed, finally reaches to turn off the light.

Fade to black.

Fade up:

EXT. AVENUE – DAY

Long shot of very sad Ted walking to work before rush hour. Melancholy music continues on the soundtrack.

> TED *(v.o.)*
> Montserrat called at eight the next morning but I had already left for the office.

Fade to black.

INT. WHISKEY BAR – DAY/TWILIGHT

A fancy whiskey bar, deserted except for the uniformed bartender and an expensively dressed, sympathetic-looking young prostitute who enters and exits while Ted and Fred talk. Both have cocktails; Ted also has a grilled cheese sandwich.

> TED
> Losing "a sale" doesn't bother me so much. I'll make other sales. But there's this thought I can't shake that's really getting me down: *Maybe I'm not cut out for sales.* I thought I liked sales and was good at it, but maybe I'm not cut out for it.

> FRED
> What exactly's the problem?

> TED
> Spending your whole life doing something you're ill suited to. Wasting your life. It's kind of depressing.

FRED

God, maybe I'm not cut out for the navy.

Fred takes a big last gulp of his drink, finishing it.

TED

I've got to get back.

FRED

You're going back to work now?

Fred looks at his watch.

FRED

For someone not cut out for something, you're pretty obsessed with it.

Ted leaves money and gets up.

TED

That doesn't mean anything.

FRED

It's, uh, okay if I stay another night?

TED

Yeah.

Dissolve to:

EXT. CENTER BARCELONA – NIGHT

Heavy evening traffic moving and not moving in downtown Barcelona, with young men and women on motorscooters trying to weave through it. Ted's voice is sad, deadened.

TED *(v.o.)*

The call from Chicago I had been dreading came that evening.

INT. TED'S OFFICE – DAY

Ted, standing, ending a phone call evidently filled with some very bad news.

TED

(*Coldly*) Okay . . . Goodbye.

He quite melodramatically puts the telephone receiver back in its cradle. Nuria looks at him with concern.

TED

That was Dickie. He's coming to Barcelona to "speak with me" and won't say what it's about – I'm getting canned.

Nuria looks at him inquiringly.

TED

Sacked. Booted. Fired. Dismissed.

NURIA

But – you're the best they have. You're a genius of sales.

TED

I'm not sure if there's such a thing as a "genius" of sales. . . . I'm not sure I'm really even cut out for sales.

NURIA

No! You're brilliant at sales, when they let you. . . .

Fade to black.

INT. TED'S APARTMENT – DAY

Ted sitting at living room table with coffee working on something when Fred comes in from the street in a great rage, carrying the morning paper.

TED (*v.o.*)

Ramon's article appeared the next day.

Fred thrusts the paper down in front of Ted. Side by side on its front page are a photo of the bombed USO building and an old newspaper engraving of the USS Maine.

TED

(*Reading-translating headline*) "Yet again? Americans themselves suspected in USO bombing."

78

FRED

. . . The most disgusting slander, incredible . . . – And where do they get this about our blowing up the *Maine?*

Ted, who seems a bit out of it, says nothing.

FRED

I'm going to the Consulate. They've got to reply to this.

Fred takes the newspaper back and starts looking at it again, enraged and incredulous.

INT. TED'S OFFICE – DAY

As Fred arrives Ted is finishing a sales telephone call with a client in Catalan. Nuria works in the background, doing something at the telex station.

TED

. . . Que mes? Molt be. Molt be. Allavorens, Dijous a las deu. Adeu siao.

FRED

(*Angry, out of breath*) God, I can't believe it –

TED

– What?

FRED

The Consul – you're not going to believe this –

TED

– What?

FRED

That half-bottle of Old Crow – the Consul accused me of stealing it!

TED

But he gave that to you.

FRED

I thought he had. He was on this interminable phone call – so I did this (*hand gestures indicating he would be taking bottle*) – and I was sure he saw me and indicated it was okay. . . .

TED

But you replaced it.

FRED

Yeah. Well, you can't find Old Crow over here, so I got a bottle of Jim Beam, which actually costs more.

TED

The bottle in the kitchen?

FRED

Yeah.

TED

But you've been drinking that.

FRED

I'm not going to replace a half-bottle of Old Crow with a full bottle of Jim Beam. I'm not an idiot.

TED

You haven't replaced it yet? Don't you see how bad that looks?

FRED

Give me a break.

TED

You know, Fred, after a while, the line between borrowing things without returning them, and theft, becomes awfully thin.

FRED

(*Furious*) Take that back!
Until you retract that, I'm not going to say another word to you.

TED

Okay . . .

FRED

What you're referring to happened twenty years ago and not at all the way you're implying. . . . Your kayak was a death ship. I almost went down in that thing. Thank God it was me – I was a stronger swimmer and able to get away. . . . I probably saved your life.

TED

Oh, great. . . . It wasn't only the kayak.

FRED

God, you're obsessed with material possessions! Maybe the Spanish are right – I mean, this American materialism is terrible. You're just like the Consul – more interested in your crummy possessions than answering the most hideously false and disgusting blood libel –

Fred holds up the newspaper again.

TED

Were you like this at the Consulate?

FRED

You know what the Consul's response is? N-o-t-h-i-n-g. He doesn't want to jeopardize his relationship with the press here.

TED

You've got to be more careful, Fred. You can't go around mouthing off this way.

FRED

Mouthing off? These are vile lies. We know how disgusting they are but no one here does. We've got to reply to this.

TED

"We"?

FRED

Yeah. I've drafted a brief letter for your signature.

He gives Ted the draft letter, which seems more like a dozen pages long. Ted starts to look at it.

FRED

You see, somebody's got to reply, and I can't.

Fred looks over his shoulder while Ted reads.

TED

(*While reading*) I don't think it's right for people in sales to get involved in matters of public controversy. . . .

FRED

"Public controversy"?

TED

(*Noticing something in letter*) I can't say their article made me "want to vomit."

FRED

Well, I'm working on that. I'll tone it down.

Ted moves to the second page and Fred takes back the first. Nuria, interested, has come closer and Fred gives her the first page to review.

FRED

Would it be okay if I asked Nuria to check the Spanish –

Ted nods "yes."

TED

(*Still reading*) – Uhn-huhn –

FRED

– I wouldn't want you to look bad.

NURIA

(*Reading*) "Vomitar"? To vomit?

FRED

Maybe that's not a good way to open. I could put it at the end.

Noticing something odd on Ted's desk, Fred picks up a piece of Ted's business correspondence to examine more closely. He looks at other papers on Ted's desk.

FRED

What are all these tiny red dots on your papers?

Ted, annoyed, pulls the paper out of Fred's hand and puts it face-down on his desk.

INT. HALLWAY/TED'S APARTMENT – NIGHT

Fred and Marta climbing the stairs in Ted's building.

> FRED
> . . . Doesn't he have some sort of problem with . . .
> impotence. . . . – It's a terrible problem.

> MARTA
> Montserrat has believed that . . .? No one has less of a problem
> of impotence than Ramon.

Fred is surprised.

> FRED
> Then what's he got against the United States?

> MARTA
> What?

*Fred, approaching the apartment and hearing the telephone ringing
inside, hurries to open the door with his key.*

TED'S APARTMENT – NIGHT

*Fred enters the darkened apartment, goes to the phone and answers it.
[Ted's answering machine's outgoing message might or might not be
triggered. If it is we might then hear Montserrat, too.]*

> FRED
> (*Into phone*) Digim.
>   Oh, hi. He's not here.

*While Fred speaks on the phone, Marta looks around the apartment,
still listening to his side of the conversation. She looks at an old photo of
a dark-haired boy grinning in a kayak on a lake, books in the
bookshelf, personal objects and other snapshots. A book of Fred's –
Mahan's* The Importance of Sea Power in History *– lies out where
he might have left it.*

> FRED
> (*On phone*) – I don't know. I just walked in. Apparently he's
> not home yet.

83

– No, he didn't say anything.
– Okay, I'll give him that message.
– Un abrazo.
– Ciao.

He hangs up the phone.

FRED

That was Montserrat. What's going on there?

Fred walks over to where Ted has hidden his foreign currency cache, carrying the pad and pencil from next to the phone.

MARTA

Ted hasn't said anything?

FRED

No. (*Thinks.*) He has been in a weird funk.

MARTA

Well, it's all his fault.

FRED

Really?

Fred opens the cache and takes out one 5,000-peseta note.

FRED

Watch: I'm taking out just one five thousand-peseta note. You're my witness.

Fred scribbles hurriedly on the pad of paper.

And I'm leaving my signed personal IOU for that amount, to be paid back within twenty-four – well, seventy-two – hours.

He finishes writing the IOU and shows it to Marta.

MARTA

Yes, it's true.

He puts the paper in with the stash.

FRED

It's actually better this way. He would have lent it to me anyway, but this spares us all the acrimony.

Fred heads toward the back of the apartment.

You don't mind waiting? I'll just be a few minutes.

MARTA

No.

Marta relaxes and strolls into the living room, looking back briefly in the direction Fred has disappeared.

EXT. TERRACE CAFÉ WITH A VIEW – NIGHT

Fred and Marta at table – serious conversation in progress.

MARTA

Ramon is very smart. That evening, one by one, he broke down all her reasons for leaving him. For instance, he has returned to writing for the newspaper's international section –

FRED

– Yeah, I know. Great. –

MARTA

He pointed out that no matter how well she and Ted were in Barcelona, at some point Ted will want to return to Chicago – which he considers the most beautiful city in the world.

FRED

(*Smiles*) I know. That's crazy. San Francisco is.

For the following, possibly also use a silent image of Ramon talking with Montserrat.

MARTA

Ramon's very persuasive and painted a terrible picture of what it would be like for her to live the rest of her life in America with its consumerism, crime and vulgarity. All those loud, badly dressed, fat people watching their eighty channels of television and visiting shopping malls. The plastic throw-everything-away society with its notorious violence and racism . . . And, finally, the total lack of culture.

FRED

It's a problem.

MARTA

Ramon was very clever because he never said anything
opposing Ted directly. He did not even mention the terrible
thing about the ants. He just pointed up how Montserrat
would be separating herself from her family and friends
forever. Even if she came back every year, her children would
grow up as Americans eating hamburgers. Finally Montserrat
was sobbing, what he was describing was so bleak.

FRED

That's pathetic. You mean she's dumped Ted and gone back
to Ramon because of some *conversation*.

MARTA

No. That is just it. She just wanted to have a serious talk with
Ted. But the way he's acted he's practically forced her into the
arms of Ramon.

FRED

She's in the arms of Ramon?

MARTA

No. I don't know.

EXT. STREET NEAR TED'S — DAY/DAWN

*Brief shot of a street deserted except for a two-man squad of orange
jumpsuited Barcelona sanitation men with a small orange sanitation
vehicle, sweeping and hosing the street. From around a corner Fred
comes into view, walking quickly, freshly showered and shaved, but lost
in thought.*

INT. TED'S APARTMENT — DAY

*Fred opens the door at Ted's, which is dark, depressing and smokey in
striking contrast to the sunny dawn outside. Ted is sitting at the
kitchen/dining room table in pyjamas and a bathrobe working on
contracts and a pile of paperwork, with an adding machine with a long
ribbon of paper coming out of it. A full ashtray and used coffee cup are
in front of him. The local version of a "golden oldies" station is on the
radio at low volume.*

FRED

(*Actually concerned*) God . . . what's going on?

TED

I'm getting canned.

FRED

But you're the best they've got. You always say so.

TED

Yeah, I know, but this jerk Dickie Taylor is calling the shots now. I don't understand how Jack could let it happen this way.

FRED

(*Actually sympathetic*) Gahd . . . and on top of the thing with Montserrat.

At mention of Montserrat Ted perceptibly slumps, hit with a wave of exhaustion and grief.

FRED

(*With concern*) Are you sure you know what you're doing there? (*Pause.*) Marta said you had practically forced Montserrat into Ramon's arms.

TED

She said that? . . . Everything was going so well. . . . She never showed up that night after going to pick up her things from Ramon's. Apparently they had talked until dawn and she ended up sleeping on his sofa – which, for all I know, is true.

FRED

Marta said he really laid it on thick on the "violence-and-racism-in-the-U.S.A." angle. And consumerism. Apparently he thinks we have too many consumer products.

TED

Ramon ranting about consumerism might depress her, but it wouldn't change everything this way. . . . Something spooked her, as if I had been crowding her. . . . And I'd really been playing it cool. . . .

A guilty look crosses Fred's face.

87

FRED

What makes you think that?

TED

Suddenly she doesn't want to move in. She wants to have a "serious talk" – you know what that means. . . .

FRED

You should at least talk to her.

TED

– No. That would be a disaster. Forever after I'd be the jerk who was crowding her whom she had to "talk to seriously."

FRED

But saying you have a work emergency –

TED

– I do have a work emergency –

FRED

– and are too busy to see her, I'm not sure –

TED

– Have you ever heard of Maneuver X?

Fred shakes his head "no."

When you get deeply into sales you find that every major transaction involves a sort of mini-identity crisis for the buyer: "A green carpet? Am I really a green carpet person?" In romance the same thing applies – but on a humongous scale. . . . That's why Maneuver X could be my only chance.

FRED

But what is Maneuver X?

TED

It's removing all pressure, creating a sort of space which the customer must affirmatively cross. Only by disappearing more thoroughly and inexplicably than Montserrat can I change the current dynamic. Will it? I don't know. I think it will. If not, I'm dead.

FRED

(*Impressed*) Wow. You've really thought this through. That's impressive. I haven't thought through anything about Marta. . . . (*A moment.*) But – isn't Maneuver X really just another way of putting what we usually refer to as "playing hard to get?"

TED

No.

FRED

Huhn.

EXT. PASEO DE GRACIA – DAY

Fred on street, nervously looking behind him. He enters the building where Ted's office is.

INT. TED'S OFFICE – DAY

Fred – in an excited, spooky state – erupts into the office where Ted and Nuria have returned to work, still in the melancholy mood that the shadow of impending doom has brought.

FRED

I'm being followed.

TED

Give me a break.

FRED

There's a guy following me. Come here, I'll show you.

Fred leads Ted over to the windows, careful to stand against the wall so he can't be seen, and as Ted approaches the window Fred gives him instructions.

(*Grabbing him back*) Not there. He'll see you. Over here, then edge your eyes around. He's on that pedestrian island, a little further down.

89

TED

He's in the car?

FRED

What car?

Fred forgets his precautions and stands in front of the window to look out. There is a car with flashing taillights illegally parked up on the sidewalk, and no man.

FRED

No, he's gone.

Ted, looking completely skeptical, walks back toward the center of the office to continue working.

FRED

There really was a guy. Wherever I went, he went.

TED

What did he look like?

FRED

. . . Sort of suspicious-looking.

TED

What was he wearing?

FRED

He was carrying something – a camera, I think.

TED

He was wearing a camera. Anything else?

FRED

I don't care what he was wearing. I'm not his fashion consultant. All I care is that he was following me.

TED

You really are far gone.

FRED

Well, if I'm far gone, then the guy following me is even farther gone.

Fred leaves, slamming the door.

EXT. AVENUE — DAY

*Ted and Fred, dressed for work, walking up Paseo de Gracia in 8 a.m.
pedestrian traffic. This morning the uniform-wearing Fred and, by
association, Ted, attract even more hostile looks than normal.*

TED

The words to pop songs are about the only literature of advice
we have on romantic matters — most of the advice very bad.

FRED

Huhn. . . . Maybe you could clarify something for me. While
I've been, you know, waiting for the fleet to show up, I've read
a lot and —

TED

— Really? —

FRED

— and one thing that keeps cropping up is this about "subtext."
Songs, novels, plays — they all have a subtext, which I take to
mean a hidden message or import of some kind.

Ted nods.

FRED

So subtext we know. But what do you call the meaning, or
message, that's right there on the surface, completely open and
obvious? They never talk about that. (*Using his hand as a visual
aid.*) What do you call what's *above* the subtext?

TED

The text.

FRED

(*Pause*) Okay. That's right. . . . But they never talk about
that.

*A guy walking in their direction reading the paper looks up and gives
Fred a look first of surprise and then withering hate.*

FRED

Jeezus, the anti-Americanism here is incredible.

91

*Fred and Ted are approaching the newspaper kiosk where they
normally buy their papers. One of its customers is standing planted on
the sidewalk reading the paper he has just bought.*

TED

Jeezus!

*The highest stack of newspapers in front of them carries the bold banner
headline: LA CIA ESTA EN BARCELONA (The CIA is in
Barcelona) above two hidden-camera style photos of Fred in Barcelona
alongside a bad-quality reproduction of his formal ROTC portrait.
They both take copies of the paper and scrutinize the front-page story
intently.*

FRED

How can they print this stuff?

*Trying to pay for the paper, Fred is treated to the undisguised anger of
the kioskero, who lets Fred's change drop to the ground so he has to
stoop to pick it up. Ted throws his copy back down on the pile and grabs
Fred by the upper arm to steer him up the street and away from a
potential incident. The newspaper reader standing near the kiosk calls
after Fred after they go:*

NEWSPAPER READER

(*With rage in his voice*) Facha!

TED

(*Turns around*) Es falso! (*Then adds:*) Imbecil!

*Fred continues walking, looking at the paper and shaking his head. Ted
has to walk faster to keep up with him.*

TED

It is false?

FRED

Of course it is. Thanks.

TED

Sorry . . .

FRED

I'm a dead man. This will kill me in the service.

92

EXT. AVENUE (LAYETANA) – DAY

*Ted in his car swings by the front door of the office building housing the U.S. Consulate. The standard two policemen with tommy guns stand in the doorway. Fred, who had been waiting in the lobby, comes out between them and (*CAR INT.*) gets in the front passenger seat. Ted pulls away quickly.*

FRED
God, that was horrible. Blame the victim. There was even a call from the Pentagon – furious . . . This has been the worst day of my life. God, that Consul's annoying.

Fred looks into the rear-view mirror.

FRED
Jesus, the white car's following us.

TED
(*Looking in the mirror*) Which white car? They're all white.

FRED
The Renault.

TED
They're all Renaults.

FRED
Cut it out. That white Renault's been tailing me all afternoon. The last thing I need is more press coverage.

He slides further down in his seat.

TED
(*Looking in the mirror*) It has Girona plates.

INT. DISCO – NIGHT

Marta returning from the disco's lounge area.

FRED
Why are you always going to the bathroom with people? I wasn't born yesterday, you know.

MARTA

You weren't born yesterday? I don't understand you. You're not in a very nice mood tonight.

FRED

You gave Ramon that information.

MARTA

I had no idea it was of significance.

FRED

Couldn't you tell I was joking? – I'm not in the CIA. It was obviously a joke.

MARTA

I have no idea what you are.

Fred sort of exhales in frustration.

FRED

You promised not to repeat to Montserrat what I said about Ted.

MARTA

About his wanting to marry her so? I had to tell her – she's my friend. She already suspected something like that anyway. She was worried about getting involved with someone who thought in such extremist terms.

FRED

Extremist?

MARTA

I think there is something fascist about a boy who immediately talks of marrying a woman he likes.

FRED

(*Hesitantly*) I don't think Ted is a fascist of the marrying kind.

Fade to black.

INT. TED'S APARTMENT — DAY/DAWN

The kitchen, where Ted has been set up most of the night working on closing contracts. Fred and Ted talking in an atmosphere of heightened drama – both are in a strange, hyper state.

FRED

You were right – something did spook her. Apparently I said something to Marta about your wanting to marry and spend the rest of your life with [her] –

TED

– But I never even told you –

FRED

– You never confide anything to me. So I have to extrapolate . . .

TED

– Why did you tell her?

FRED

– It seemed interesting. You're in a conversation, it has this momentum, you want to tell the other person interesting or funny things, and you end up telling things that, on reflection, maybe you shouldn't.

TED

It was just some "funny thing" –

FRED

– I'm sorry. You were right. I'd take it back if I could. Montserrat's gone to Paris to take the summer program at the Institute.

Ted leans forward on the table and rests his head on his hands.

FRED

It was all my fault. I'm sorry.

Ted stays in the same position, saying nothing.

> FRED

I'm not sure if this is the right time to mention this – well, I
know it's not – but . . . I think I might be in love with
Montserrat too. She's fantastic.

Ted looks up, incredulous.

> FRED

What if you and Montserrat are *not* perfect for each other,
what if Montserrat and I am? Am I supposed to give up any
possibility of happiness, of ever knowing whether she was
precisely the one person in the world I was meant to be with,
just because of the accident you met her first?

> TED

(*Convincingly*) I could slit your throat.

> FRED

So could I. (*Long pause.*) I'll never mention it again.

*Fred turns and walks away while Ted stays at the table, shaking his
head, still furious.*

INT. TED'S LIVING ROOM – DAY

*Early-morning light is pouring in and the mood has improved a lot.
Ted, showered and dressed for work, walks across the room to his multi-
national currencies stash.*

> TED

I've got to go to Milan this morning but I'm thinking of going
up to Paris Monday. There's some IHSMOCO business I
should take care of there.

> FRED

Will you call Montserrat before you go?

> TED

I think I'll just call her when I'm there. Play it somewhat cool.

FRED

You're keeping on with Maneuver X?

TED

Yeah, a modified X.

Ted works on opening his well-hidden currency stash.

FRED

Oh, I forgot: I borrowed five thousand pesetas the other night.
Would it be okay if I paid you later?

TED

You have this very bad habit of borrowing things without
informing the lender.

FRED

Uh, sorry about that. . . .

*Ted carefully opens his stash. There is nothing in it – at least several
thousand dollars in Spanish and other European currencies is missing –
the only item left is Fred's IOU.*

TED

(*Reads note*) "IOU five thousand pesetas to be paid back within
X twenty-four X seventy-two hours. – Fred."
So you've passed over to real larceny.

FRED

(*Upset and very worried*) I didn't take it. I just took one peseta
bill. The rest was all there.

TED

I don't care. That's enough.

FRED

You can't believe I'd really steal.

TED

How does it look?

Fred, his face flushed with shame and rage, goes to his room.

INT. FRED'S ROOM – DAY

Fred packing his navy duffle bag with suppressed emotion. Perhaps while packing Fred realizes what happened to the money, which does not lessen his depression.

INT. TED'S APARTMENT – DAY

Ten minutes later, Ted stands near his former cash stash with a mechanical pencil and paper, making a list. Fred comes out of his room in full uniform under a raincoat, carrying his duffle bag. He puts down the bag to put on his hat.

> FRED
> I'll either get your money or pay you back myself.

Ted walks over and gives Fred the paper. Fred looks at it and shakes his head grimly.

> FRED
> Jeezus.

Fred walks to the door, Ted walks after him, as if to make certain that he goes. Fred opens the door and then turns around.

> FRED
> I don't steal. I didn't take your money. You've always been so self-righteous towards me – since we were ten years old – it's really unbearable.

> TED
> (*Pointedly*) What happened when we were ten? You're such a liar.

Fred, who's as low as he can go psychologically, gives him a terrible look.

EXT. CITY STREET – DAY

Fred, in grim state, walking along the sidewalk of a street like Layetana in gloomy weather carrying his duffle bag and other things. The white Renault with Gerona plates drives slowly, slightly behind him, then speeds up, passing him.

INT. MARTA'S BUILDING – DAY

Fred in Marta's building with his baggage going up elevator or approaching the apartment door. He knocks and there is no answer, so he extracts a key and opens the door.

INT. MARTA'S APARTMENT – DAY

Fred drops his bags and walks to a table where there are all sorts of envelopes and packets, some containing whitish powder or blocks of dried herbs, but others with foreign currency. Fred picks up the foreign currency envelopes but, before he can check them, is surprised by sounds from the bedroom. He walks over to the bedroom doorway and sees Marta and a guy he recognizes as one of her disco-lounge-area pals having intercourse on the mattress at the other end of the room, each with their hands over the other's ears. Fred walks back to the salon with a Stan Laurel-like expression, picks up his things, including the money, and leaves.

INT. STAIRWAY – DAY

Fred walks down the stairs carrying his things. The door opening and footsteps can be heard above.

MARTA (o.s.)

Fred . . . Fred . . .

She leans over the railing and looks down.

MARTA

Fred . . .

Toward the bottom of the stairs, Fred stops a moment.

FRED

Oh – sorry.

He throws the key up the stairwell and it falls clankingly on the landing near her.

EXT. STREET — DAY

Fred gets into a cab with his duffle bag and other possessions.

FRED
(*Out of breath*) Paseo de Gracia, diez y seis, por favor.

INT./EXT. TAXI CAB — DAY

Inside the cab Fred, ostensibly in a very good mood, recites his self-improvement motto to himself.

FRED
Every day, in every way, I am becoming a better and better lieutenant junior grade. Every day, in every way, I am becoming a better and better lieutenant junior grade.

Fred chuckles to himself and looks out the left window, where a motorcycle carrying a grim-looking driver and passenger pulls even with the taxi and keeps pace with it. The barrel of a gun juts from the passenger's clothing, pointing at Fred. Fred looks up into the face of the gunman staring at him; his expression as the gunman shoots; the gun blast, the taxi window smashing, blood splattering across the taxi's interior, and Fred's form slumping at the edge of the frame; a quick fade to black, mixed with red. Dreadful sound effects: "keening Arab women" run backward and "high-pitched shriek" run slowly.

ARMED FORCES MONTAGE

The dreadful sound effects dissolve into the heavy rhythm of Johnny Cash's "I Walk the Line" and we are in a different world, a montage focusing on the lonely aspects of the life of American servicemen overseas, with a heavy emphasis on the Sixth Fleet and the navy, and the everyday images of sailors on chowline or on duty, becoming interspersed with grim images of American military victims of foreign terrorism such as the bombing of the marine barracks in Beirut.

FRED-TED HOSPITAL MONTAGE

The Johnny Cash song or melancholy original theme music link a series of dolly shots ending with a guilty-looking, preoccupied Ted in the hospital where the comatose and maimed Fred is being treated.

EXT. AVENUE — DAY/TWILIGHT

Police antiterrorist roadblock and checkpoint in downtown Barcelona, with a huge traffic tie-up behind it.

EXT. HOSPITAL — DAY/TWILIGHT

Ted running from taxi to hospital, where there is heavy security. (Establish the security presence at the hospital where possible, national police with tommy guns, and initially some press, though this is kept minor.)

INT. HOSPITAL LOBBY/RECEPTION — DAY/TWILIGHT

Ted rushing around the hospital reception area trying to find out how and where Fred is, and to get access to him.

INT. HOSPITAL ICU MONTAGE — TWILIGHT/NIGHT

Inside the hospital operating room: montage of insert shots showing detail of ICU and operating room procedure, machines: the bloody bandages and instruments on the side of the operating table; Fred's almost lifeless wrist with hospital ID bracelet; machine monitoring heart/brain function, etc.

INT. HOSPITAL ICU AREA — NIGHT

Ted waiting, walking, in area where visitors are normally off-limits, looking through glass panels, down a corridor, to a partial view of the bloody hubbub that is the intensive care unit/emergency room; an occasional orderly or nurse rushes in or out with needed materials, one with a bloodstained white jacket. Some security forces are around. A doctor comes out of the surgery, his surgical uniform covered in blood and human crud, looking shattered and exhausted, and notices Ted.

TED (*v.o.*)
Even if Fred survived, his doctors had no idea what degree of normality he might be able to resume.

INT. HOSPITAL CORRIDOR—NIGHT

Ted walking alongside as an orderly wheels the bed carrying a mummy-like Fred with IV units back to his room, perhaps a hideous wound on his shaved head partly visible.

TED
(*To inert Fred:*) You're going to be okay. I'm going to stay with you, man.

INT. FRED'S ROOM – NIGHT

Ted sitting in Fred's room watching him, though the only signs of life are erratic breathing and weird twitching.

TED (*v.o.*)
Even the disasters that strike those we are closest to only reach us filtered through our own colossal egotism. My response to what happened to Fred was swamped in subjective emotion – mostly guilt. I prayed for him all the time but with the constant doubt that I was probably just kidding myself – I was beginning to suspect my religious faith was largely bogus.

During the above, just before "I prayed," Ted closes his eyes and slumps forward with his elbows on his knees and his hands clenched together as if praying.

TED (*v.o.*)
I resolved to stay there all the time and do whatever I possibly could to improve Fred's chances for recovery.

— Ted bolting up from his chair to check an IV unit; he stares at it as it nears the "empty" mark and then presses the "nurse call" button. (A nurse with a fresh IVU enters the room.)

INT. HOSPITAL PHONE BANK — DAY

Ted, finishing a phone call, notices Fred's doctor passing by on his way out of the hospital. Ted hurriedly follows him out.

EXT. OUTSIDE HOSPITAL — DAY

The doctor is met by his wife driving an expensive car, with their two young daughters and miscellaneous summer baggage in the back. Ted and the doctor speak (initially silent under voice-over) as his wife walks around to the passenger side.

> TED (*v.o.*)
> Fred was shot just before one of the long summer weekends. By late Friday the hospital's entire senior medical staff seemed to have disappeared.

> TED
> (*To the doctor:*) I can't believe you're just going. There must be something more you can do.

> DR. RIBO
> Don't worry ("*Dant gworrie*"). Your buddy will get the best medicine care.

INT. HOSPITAL — DAY

Ted returns to the room and Fred's bed is not there; Ted is hurrying down halls looking for Fred.

(Soundtrack: Dr. Ribo's words — "dant gworrie," "dant gworrie" — ringing in Ted's ears with distortion or echo effect.)

> TED (*v.o.*)
> For me "don't worry" is the most frightening phrase in the English language — "dant gworrie" even more so. It almost invariably means *they're* not going to worry, but *you* better had.

103

INT. HOSPITAL — DAY

Ted passes through one landing where an orderly is smoking a cigarette, in the next deserted hallway finds Fred abandoned in his IVU-strewn bed.

                    TED
  Jeezus.

Ted runs back to the landing.

INT. HOSPITAL CORRIDOR — NIGHT

Ted, furious, walking alongside red-faced orderly pushing Fred's bed down corridor.

                    TED (*v.o.*)
  Each hour Fred remained unconscious his chances apparently got worse.

INT. HOSPITAL TELEPHONE BANK — NIGHT

Ted speaking emphatically on a phone, having trouble making himself heard long distance.

                    TED (*v.o.*)
  Fred's parents were impossible to locate.

                    TED
  (*On phone*) Why would they want to do that?

                    TED (*v.o.*)
  It turned out they'd gone on some stupid photo safari to New Zealand.

Ted looking pretty upset.

INT. HOSPITAL CORRIDOR — NIGHT

An agitated, determined Ted walking down a hospital corridor at a fast pace.

                                TED
Get a grip. Get a grip. Get a grip.

INT. FRED'S ROOM, HOSPITAL — NIGHT

Ted keeping a vigil at Fred's bedside, pacing and talking.

                            TED (*v.o.*)
I'd heard that the sound of familiar voices could help, so I
tried to keep up a steady stream of chatter in Fred's room –

                                TED
(*Chattering, pacing*) . . . and then Charlie Johnson said, "But
she . . ."

                            TED (*v.o.*)
– and to arrange an around-the-clock vigil of friends to read to
him. But it was hard finding books in English in Barcelona that
Fred might like.

INT. — FRED'S ROOM, LATER — NIGHT

Ted sitting near Fred's bed reading aloud from a paperback.

                                TED
"We seek him here, we seek him there,
Those Frenchies seek him everywhere.
Is he in heaven? – Is he in hell?
That demmed, elusive Pimpernel?"

Ted looks at Fred to see if he has any reaction, but he doesn't.

INT. HOSPITAL PHONE BANK — NIGHT

Ted talking in intense tones on the phone.

                            TED (*v.o.*)
What was really disillusioning was how some people let you
down when someone gets sick.

                                105

TED

(*Leaving message on answering machine*) It's eight thirty. The situation's really bad. I don't understand why you haven't come yet. You're really needed here. . . .

INT. FRED'S ROOM, HOSPITAL — NIGHT

TED (*v.o.*)

Aurora Boval turned out to be a real trouper.

Image of cheerful Aurora arriving in room with flowers, provisions, and books in English such as A Tale of Two Cities *or* War and Peace. *She kisses Ted on the cheek and goes over to Fred and kisses him too.*

TED (*v.o.*)

Marta never showed up.

INT. HOSPITAL RECEPTION AREA — DAY

Ted with some navy officers and American officials.

TED (*v.o.*)

The Naval Attache flew in from Madrid and the Consul was there almost immediately. He turned out to be a great guy, terrific with the hospital administration. He couldn't believe Fred had taken the thing about the Old Crow bottle seriously.

CONSUL

I was just kidding. I forgot guys who joke around a lot can be so sensitive themselves. I have no sense of humor, so he must have assumed I was being serious. . . .

TED (*v.o.*)

Among the plainclothes navy guards assigned to the hospital was our friend Frank, who in his off-duty hours helped me with the reading.

Frank in the chair next to Fred's bed reading from a thick paperback.

FRANK

(*Reading somewhat awkwardly*) "She stopped, seeing in her

106

husband's glowing eyes the rage she had herself experienced after his duel with Dolohov.

"'Wherever you are, there is vice and evil,' said Pierre to his wife. 'Anatole, come with me! I must speak with you,' he added in French."

INT. FRED'S ROOM, LATER – NIGHT

Ted alone in room sitting near Fred's bed keeping watch over him. Occasionally Fred blinks or his body makes involuntary movements while he remains in the coma.

TED (*v.o.*)

Sometimes it seemed as if Fred were already dead, leaving just his maimed, still-breathing body behind.

Fred and I didn't hate each other our whole childhood. The summer we were ten there was a thirty-six-hour period we were on quite good terms. After we both cut ourselves in a freak fishing accident we even took advantage of all the blood to become "blood brothers."

EXT. THE LAKE – DAY

Possible flashback of Fred and Ted as ten-year-olds on floating dock on the lake, one of them losing control of a fishing rod on the upswing with the hook flying around and both trying to dodge or fend it off with their hands; blood-brothers procedure; then young Ted paddling away in nifty though battered kayak, with young Fred watching.

TED (*v.o.*)

Later that afternoon I went into town with my parents. I never saw my kayak again.

An agitated nurse enters the room, interrupting Ted's revery.

NURSE I

Hay una mujer aqui que insiste en hablar con usted. (*There's a woman here who insists on speaking to you.*)

TED

Conmigo? (*With me?*)

NURSE I

Si.

The nurse leaves the room, looking at her watch, preoccupied. Ted follows her out, briefly glancing at his watch too.

INT. HOSPITAL CORRIDOR/RECEPTION – NIGHT

Ted and the nurse walk hurriedly down the hall.

In a reverie, Ted sees Montserrat turning around, her face a heartbreaking combination of profound concern, love, wistful regret, sweetness and hope.

At the other end of the corridor, in the reception area, a young woman stands with her back to them – but clearly not Montserrat. As Ted approaches, she turns around and it's Marta.

TED

Oh, hi.

INT. HOSPITAL, FRED'S ROOM – NIGHT

Marta leaning over Fred, stroking his face with her hand. She kisses his face and starts to leave. Ted stands some distance away. Aurora and another girl from the trade fair, dressed in identical modish red outfits from one of the fair's stands, come forward from the other side of the room.

TED

We can go out. You'd probably like to stay with him alone for a while.

MARTA

No. Actually, I'm here to see you.

TED

It's about Fred?

MARTA

No.

Ted starts escorting Marta out.

108

TED

I'll walk you out.

AURORA

(*To Ted:*) You should go home for a sleep – you look so tired.

Ted doesn't react, as if too tired to think fast.

Greta and I can stay here. Greta has a very good English and loves this book.

Ted looks at them. GRETA *nods and smiles reservedly.*

TED

Okay . . . thanks.

Ted walks back to Fred's bed and looks down at him. An involuntary movement of Fred's while still comatose surprises them. His twitches and sudden unconscious movements cast a creepy pall over the room.

TED

There's still hope, you know. . . . I mean more than hope. He could come out of it any time and be basically okay, with very little . . . consequences, or very few.

He leans closer to Fred.

TED

Fred . . . Fred.

There is no response. Ted turns around. Aurora has the paperback open trying to find for Greta the place where Ted left off reading. She passes the book to Ted and he picks out exactly where he left off.

TED

Here.

He passes the book back to Greta, holding the place open for her.

GRETA

(*Reading*) " 'That man is somehow . . .' "?

TED

Yeah.

After cheek-kissing, Ted and Marta leave, Greta looking after them a moment and then down at Fred.

GRETA

Que lastima.

AURORA

Si.

Greta, sitting in the chair next to Fred's bed with the book, looks at him a moment longer and then starts reading.

GRETA

" 'That man is somehow closely and painfully connected with me,' thought Prince Andrei. Suddenly he remembered Natasha as he had seen her for the first time at the ball in 1810, with her slender neck and arms, and with her frightened, happy face ready for rapture . . .' "

EXT. RESIDENTIAL STREET — NIGHT

Ted walks Marta from the hospital in a quiet, tree-lined, residential neighborhood to where she left her motorcycle.

TED

Fifteen minutes don't go by that I don't think of her. I think about her all the time.

MARTA

That's too bad. I thought you had gotten over her.

TED

What do you mean?

MARTA

It was impossible. You had no chance.

TED

Why do you say that?

MARTA

It's only my opinion. . . . When Fred was shot did he have envelopes of cash money with him?

                          TED

Yes.

                         MARTA

That money is mine and I need it back.

                          TED

What?

                         MARTA

I need that money back. I'm going on a journey.

                          TED

That money was taken from me. Fred was just recovering it.

                         MARTA

You suspect me of having taken that money.

                          TED

I'm sorry. You didn't take it?

                         MARTA

I did, but it was only three thousand dollars. When Fred came
he took more than those.

                          TED

(*Coldly*) What do you want?

                         MARTA

I want the money that belongs to me.

                          TED

(*Glacial*) How much is that?

                         MARTA

Two thousand dollars! I need that money. I am going away.

                          TED

(*Skeptically*) Where?

                         MARTA

The Maldive Islands.

                          TED

The Maldives?

MARTA

(*Emotional*) I am decided to change my life, for completely.
But I need that money. . . . (*Pause.*) From now on, I want to
lead an exemplary life.

TED

Exemplary?

Marta, emotional, nods her head "yes."

TED

What about Fred?

MARTA

Fred shall not want to see me. Something shameful happened.
He didn't tell you? And I think the one Fred truly liked was
Montserrat, though he'd never tell you so.

EXT. BARCELONA STREETS — NIGHT

*A taxi speeding down avenue late at night with Ted looking out, sad.
Sad orchestral music begins.*

INT. HOSPITAL RECEPTION AREA — NIGHT

*Nurses working on the night shift when suddenly the sound of a girl's
scream comes from the direction of Fred's room. All or most of the nurses
on duty run toward his room.*

INT. TED'S APARTMENT — NIGHT

*The music continues. Shots of objects belonging to Fred – souvenirs,
snapshots, books (*The Importance of Sea Power in History, *by
Admiral Mahan), etc. Ted sleeps sprawled fully dressed on the sofa, the
light on and some business-related reading material next to him. The
telephone is ringing. Ted drags himself up to a sitting position to answer
the phone.*

TED

Diga.

A woman on the other end gives him apparently alarming news.

112

EXT. STREET NEAR TED'S – NIGHT

Ted hurriedly crosses a deserted plaza and flags down a passing cab, which stops with squealing tires. The music continues.

INT. HOSPITAL – NIGHT/DAWN

In the hospital reception area, Greta, the cool trade-fair girl Aurora brought with her, is in tears. Ted looks somber. The sad music gets sadder. The nurses in the area look subdued, too. From the far end of the corridor, Dr. Ribo comes into view, walking toward them with a somber expression. The trade-fair girl sobs. Ted puts an arm around her.

> TED
> It's not your fault. You did everything right. . . . It was very good you were there.

A distant view of Dr. Ribo approaching Ted and the girl, and then the two of them listening somberly as he talks.

Cut to:

A two-shot of Ted and the girl listening to Dr. Ribo with concern.

> TED
> . . . Couldn't you have anticipated that?

> DR. RIBO
> An infection of this nature could derive from foreign matters entering the wound during the accident –

> TED
> – the shooting –

> DR. RIBO
> – the shooting, for which we administered massive antibiotics. But maybe these have not been effective.

INT. HOSPITAL, FRED'S ROOM – DAY

Fred in his bed breathing less regularly, surrounded by more hospital machinery and IVU attachments, with a tube down his throat. Greta is

113

slumped back in one of the white plastic hospital armchairs, looking concerned. Ted is in a hard chair next to Fred's bed, leaning forward close to him.

> TED
>
> (*Whispering to Fred:*) Can you hear anything, man? . . . If you can pull out of this, you could rest up at the Lake for the rest of the summer. . . . Try to think about the Lake.

After a moment Ted gets down on his knees next to Fred's bed, as if preparing to pray, but something causes him to delay. He looks back at Greta.

> TED
>
> Do you mind, I feel sort of awkward with someone looking on.

> GRETA
>
> What?

> TED
>
> I was going to uh . . . say something and – it's sort of awkward.

She still doesn't get it.

> TED
>
> It'll only be five or ten minutes.

He waits for her to leave.

> GRETA
>
> No, I'm sorry . . .

She gets up, but instead of leaving the room, gets on her knees next to Ted.

> TED
>
> Oh, well, okay. . . . You know some Catholic prayer?

Greta gives him an uncomprehending look.

INT. HOSPITAL, FRED'S ROOM – DAY

Some time later, Ted paces the room, stopping to lean over and look with a preoccupied expression at Fred, who is not doing well. Ted continues pacing. Greta sits back in the armchair, observing him.

GRETA

Are you the boy who wanted to marry Montserrat? –

TED

(*Quickly*) – No.

He continues pacing, but thinking over Greta's question.

TED

Who told you that?

GRETA

What?

TED

That I wanted to marry Montserrat.

GRETA

There was just this story of an American boy who fell in love with Montserrat and decided he wanted to marry and spend the rest of his life with her the night they met, while they were dancing to a Bee Gees song. (*Indicating Fred.*) Is he the boy who was in love with Montserrat?

TED

No, I don't think so.

GRETA

But Montserrat does know you – she called after you left and asked about both of you.

TED

What did she say?

GRETA

I don't know. Aurora took the message.

INT. HOSPITAL, FRED'S ROOM – DAY

Some time later, Ted finishes a cup of coffee in hospital chinaware, a tray from the cafeteria. Greta is occupied, drawing with a pencil in a spiral-bound sketchbook.

115

TED

Why weren't you in that article on the most beautiful women of the trade fair?

GRETA

(*Smiles*) You thought I should be there?

TED

Sure.

GRETA

I loathe that fellow. Do you know him?

TED

We've met. That's interesting you loathe him – how come?

GRETA

I don't have the English but in Castilian we would say he is "repelente."

TED

"Repellant." That's good. . . . What's your name?

GRETA

Greta.

TED

That's not very Catalan.

GRETA

I'm not Catalan.

Ted takes a look at Greta's drawing. It is impressively executed in nineteenth-century black-and-white pen-and-ink style but with a very odd content: Fred unconscious in his hospital bed with four large-winged old-fashioned male angels standing guard over him at the four corners of his bed and a praying figure on his knees in front of the bed. Ted looks at the bed to compare it to the drawing.

TED

Who's this?

Ted indicates the praying figure on his knees. Greta glances up at him with a smile.

116

                              TED

Are you religious?

                             GRETA

Quasi.

                              TED

Do you want to be an artist?

                             GRETA

No.

Greta's exhaustion is finally catching up with her. She momentarily slumps with tiredness.

                              TED

Listen, you should get some rest.

                             GRETA

You think I should go?

                              TED

Well . . .

                             GRETA

I could stay longer if you like. Until Aurora comes – (*looks closely at watch*) – she's retarded.

                              TED

Actually I was thinking of sacking out here.

He indicates the sofa.

                             GRETA

Sacking OUT?

                              TED

Sleeping here – maybe on the sofa.

Greta gets up, now allowing herself to show her tiredness and yawn.

                             GRETA

Do you really think he will become well – are you convinced of that?

TED

Yes . . .

Greta walks closer to Fred's bed to take a last look at how he's doing before leaving.

TED

It was really great you were here last night. Thanks for staying.

Greta looks at Ted long and intently.

Fade to black.

INT. HOSPITAL, FRED'S ROOM – TWILIGHT/EARLY EVENING

The lights are off, shades drawn, and it's quite dark outside. Ted is sprawled on the sofette, asleep, next to the book he was reading aloud. A wedge of light opens from the door. Ted sits up, embarrassed to have a nurse find him sacked out during the day, groggily rubbing his eyes, still half asleep. At first he doesn't take in it's Montserrat and not hospital staff at the door. Montserrat starts walking quietly across the room.

TED

Oh, hi.

MONTSERRAT

Hi. I'm sorry I didn't come more soon – I only heard yesterday.

TED

You only heard yesterday?

Montserrat nods.

MONTSERRAT

Is he any better?

Ted shakes his head "no," quite broken up. He gets up and stands next to Fred's bed, looking down on him. Montserrat stands next to him.

TED

There were all these things I blew way out of proportion – things that seemed crimes at the time but were really of no

118

importance whatsoever. Fred was right – I persecuted him for trivialities. Maybe he did save my life, going down in the kayak that way. . . .

Montserrat, very sad, in a comradely gesture puts her arm around Ted and leans her head against him. Ted, quite far gone too, pauses a moment before continuing. Cut to a close-up of Fred's face in coma, with Montserrat and Ted only partly visible out of focus in the background.

TED *(partially o.s.)*
Even those board scores – that couldn't have been right. Before that I always assumed Fred was smarter than I was. . . . – Well, maybe not smarter, but . . .

The closeup of Fred reveals his one good eye popping open in apparent consciousness after Ted says the part about him being "smarter," then closing again, both unseen by the others.

TED
Maybe his explanation was true. . . .

Montserrat looks at Ted expectantly.

TED
Fred said that when he was taking the boards this incredibly annoying girl sat next to him who kept adjusting and fiddling with her brassiere. . . . (*Ted imitates the supposed girl fidgeting with her bra.*) Fred went to an all-boys school and found her fidgeting so annoying and distracting he lost his place on the answer sheet [and] –

MONTSERRAT
– You thought that was not true?

TED
Well, I always assumed it was false.

At a couple of points as Ted talks, Fred's eye opens with a weird or puzzled look, and closes again. Finally, with his eye closed, he turns over, as he has many times before while unconscious. Montserrat, thinking this is a positive sign, turns dramatically to Ted, with a hopeful expression.

TED

(*Regretfully*) No, that's the way it's been. He moves and you think "he's come out of it!" – but he hasn't.

A pause.

MONTSERRAT

Should we go somewhere to talk?

TED

Until Fred comes out of this, I kind of made a resolution not to do or think about anything else. . . . (*Pause, looks at watch.*) Maybe when Aurora comes . . .

MONTSERRAT

– We came together. They're in the cafeteria. I'll get them.

Montserrat turns to go out the door.

TED

I'll stay here with Fred.

Ted looks after her for a time, then carefully closes the door, walks over to Fred's bed and gets on his knees to pray.

TED

Our Father, Who art in Heaven, please forgive us our sins and *please* bring Fred back to full consciousness with all his mental capabilities and everything reasonably intact. Please forgive my doubting, vainglory and unworthiness as I make this plea that my cousin, Fred –

FRED (*o.s.*)

– Oh – give – me – a – break.

Fred's voice is weak and creaky, but emphatic. Ted, dumbstruck with joy, rises to examine his face but initially sees nothing to indicate Fred has returned to consciousness. Then, after Ted stares at his inexpressive face for a few moments, Fred's eye suddenly bugs out in a fierce-fish look of hostility and infantile petulance, then closes again.

TED

Fred! You're back.

INT. HOSPITAL CORRIDOR — NIGHT

Ted excitedly appears in the hallway, calls "doctor" once in each direction, and disappears back into Fred's room. For a while the corridor remains empty, except for a couple of nurses farther down the hall, who slowly begin to react to Ted's commotion. Then Ted reappears in the same ecstatic rushing-around state, a bit like Snoopy in one of his manic episodes, this time approaching the nurses and speaking to them quickly in Spanish. He then catches sight of Montserrat, Aurora and her friend Greta coming down the hall.

                         TED
Fred esta bien.

The three start hurrying down the hallway. One of the nurses goes for a doctor and the other hurries with Ted back into Fred's room.

INT. FRED'S ROOM, HOSPITAL — NIGHT

Ted stands alongside Fred's bed trying to keep him alert, questioning him, while Fred hovers in a strange state just within consciousness, though at some points drifting out. For Ted it's like trying to converse with someone who is partly asleep. The young doctor and a nurse are with Ted. Frank, Aurora, Montserrat, and Greta wait just outside the half-closed door, intently trying to follow how things are going but too far away to really hear all of it.

                         TED
How much can you remember?

Ted tries to keep in eye and whisper contact with the doctor to follow his indications. After listening to the doctor's brief, whispered advice, Ted nods and continues.

                         TED
Do you remember who I am?

Fred just looks at him, saying nothing.

                         TED
Do you remember who I am?

121

FRED

(*Peevish*) Yes.

TED

Who am I?

FRED

Some civilian.

TED

Who am I?

FRED

Oh, what do I care!

Fred petulantly turns his head or body and closes his eyes in a quest for sleep. Ted turns to the doctor with a near-joyous expression.

TED

This is terrific – he's going to have a complete recovery.

INT. HOSPITAL CORRIDOR – NIGHT

Outside Fred's room, Ted, still in near-ecstatic state, confers with the young doctor. The others gather near them.

TED

But it's amazing. . . . This is really good.

The doctor tries to look cheerful, slightly nods his head but hesitates in saying anything.

TED

It looks like his recovery's going to be absolutely complete, wouldn't you say?

DOCTOR

Yyess.
    His memory . . . (*Moves hand indicating fluctuation.*)

TED

But over the long term . . .

DOCTOR

Yyess, over the long term . . .

TED

I mean, it looks like his recovery's going to be absolutely complete. . . .

The doctor smiles and nods his head cheerfully but noncommittally.

INT. CAFÉ NEAR HOSPITAL – NIGHT/LATE TWILIGHT

Montserrat and Ted sit at a small table in the back of the café. Ted talks, Montserrat smokes.

TED

I'm really happy. It looks really good.

MONTSERRAT

I was concerned he didn't seem to remember your name.

TED

(*Lightly*) Well . . . it's not a very memorable name. . . . I'm just really relieved he seems basically okay.

MONTSERRAT

Yes.

TED

It looked really bad for a while. I was quite bitter about you and Marta. . . . I think you really acted badly.

MONTSERRAT

(*Surprised*) What?

TED

You must have heard before yesterday – it was in all the newspapers.

MONTSERRAT

I would have come immediately. I really like Fred.

Ted still looks skeptical.

MONTSERRAT

I'm not lying . . .

Ted and Montserrat turn their heads to look toward the door briefly.

123

Greta enters the café and walks to the bar to place an order without looking in their direction.

MONTSERRAT

What happened?

TED

You went to get your "music" – and never came back.

MONTSERRAT

But it was you! You wouldn't even talk with me.

Greta looks in their direction, sees them in intense conversation, and looks elsewhere.

TED

That was just Maneuver X.

Montserrat gives him a blank look.

TED

Our being together was never anything you'd decided affirmatively. As it was never the result of an affirmative decision on your part –

MONTSERRAT

– You had made an affirmative decision?

Ted nods "yes." Greta stands around waiting for her order in the background, looking a bit awkward.

MONTSERRAT

I really just wanted to get my "music."

TED

The long conversations would have followed –

MONTSERRAT

– Except you wouldn't talk to me. –

TED

– That was Maneuver X. If someone in a relationship wants more space – give them more space than they ever dreamed of. . . . But apparently it doesn't always work.

MONTSERRAT

I think maybe it did work.

Ted looks at Montserrat, trying to figure out if her comment is as positive as it seems. Greta, finally leaving with her order, exchanges a quick wave with them before going out.

MONTSERRAT

You know Aurora's friend?

TED

Yes.

MONTSERRAT

She's very pretty.

TED

(*Very strongly*) She's great.

MONTSERRAT

People say she's quite odd.

Ted looks surprised and somewhat annoyed.

MONTSERRAT

She's always wearing hats and making these drawings with angels and devils in the background. . . . I think she could be Opus.

TED

Opus Dei? No. She said she was only "quasi" religious. (*Pause.*) That's quite an indictment – she wears hats.

Montserrat laughs.

MONTSERRAT

No, I like her. But not her hats.

INT. TED'S BEDROOM – NIGHT

Montserrat removes herself from under covers and Ted's arm. She puts a shirt over her shoulders and starts getting up, trying to be quiet and not awake Ted, but he wakes up anyway.

                              MONTSERRAT
You fell asleep.

Ted bolts up and starts throwing on his clothes.

                                 TED
Damn . . .

Ted looks at his watch and shakes his head while hurrying to get dressed.

                                 TED
It's so typical of this guy to make me meet him at the airport.

Montserrat looks confused.

                                 TED
Dickie Taylor, the terrible guy from marketing, has set it up so I have to rush out to the airport to get fired.

                              MONTSERRAT
(*Sympathetic*) I can't believe that. They're crazy.

                                 TED
I don't know. I've been having all these doubts. . . . Could you stay at the hospital with Fred until I get back?

After a moment of non-comprehension, Montserrat nods "yes."

EXT./INT. TED IN CAB ON HIGHWAY – DAY

Ted in a cab rushing to the airport.

EXT. BARCELONA AIRPORT, APPROACHING INT. TERMINAL – DAY

Cab pulling up to terminal and Ted getting out.

INT. BARCELONA AIRPORT, INTERNATIONAL TERMINAL – DAY

Dickie Taylor looks the preppie, "terrible-Yalie" asshole marketing genius Ted described. He is tall, good-looking, expensively overdressed with his hair slicked back wet. He and Ted walk together in the terminal building, talking. Ted's face is full of resentment.

DICKIE

Thanks for coming out. I'm sorry to set it up this way but the only connecting flight's at eleven.

INT. AIRPORT CAFETERIA – DAY

Generic Spanish airport cafeteria of the old style. Waiters in white jackets and black straight ties. Dickie and Ted sit at a square steel and formica table with coffee, croissants, and bottles of Schweppes "Naranja." Dickie seems very somber.

DICKIE

I should get to what I'm here for. . . . I'm afraid I've some really bad news.

TED

It is bad news?

DICKIE

Yeah.

TED

I thought so. . . . Listen, Dickie, let's make this a lot easier: I quit. *(Angrily.)* I don't understand why Jack couldn't call and tell me himself. It's not right –

DICKIE

– What are you talking about? Jack's sick. He's gonna die.

TED

What?

DICKIE

Jack's sick.

TED

This isn't one of your sick marketing jokes?

DICKIE

No. . . . It's really bad.

Ted is stunned.

TED

I can't believe it. . . . Jack's such a great guy.

DICKIE

Yeah. The whole company's devastated. Jack is the last of the greats.

TED

(*Devastated*) He's such a great guy.

DICKIE

Yeah. He is. . . . I'll admit I always resented the incredible favoritism he showed you.

TED

There was no favoritism.

DICKIE

Oh, come on. . . . Anyway. Jack's very worried about the company. Dwight and Ron are older than Jack and, with Tom Gray gone, there's no "middle generation" to succeed them. Jack's afraid that left to itself the board might bring in an outsider with no idea what makes IHSMOCO so extraordinary – which would be a disaster.

TED

Yeah.

DICKIE

Jack asked me whom in our class I could work with best – naturally I mentioned you. It's great the feedback you've given us in marketing – it's had a critical dimension, but basically I think you're right. This idea of marketing as a science is pure myth.

Ted is very surprised.

DICKIE

Jack said, "Great" – apparently this was just his plan. The full board meets Tuesday and he's going to propose that Ron and Dwight stay on while you and I handle operations. He wants pledges from both of us to stay with the company at least five years. And he wants you back in Chicago as soon as possible.

TED

I thought you were here to fire me.

DICKIE

Yeah, what was all that "I quit" stuff about – for a moment I thought . . .

TED

(*With residual animosity*) Well, I'm way behind those sales targets you set.

DICKIE

I didn't set them – Jack did.

TED

What?

DICKIE

You don't know Jack's theory about you? He thinks that basically you aren't cut out for sales – that it's not your life's work – but that as long as you think you're behind you'd struggle to keep up and not worry whether you're really "cut out" for it or not.

TED

Jack doesn't think I'm cut out for sales?

DICKIE

No, not the way Henry or someone like him is.

TED

But . . . selling is more than just a job one's cut out or not cut out for. It's a culture, a whole way of thinking about experience – bringing to bear all the insights of Carnegie and Bettger –

DICKIE

– Listen, we all like Carnegie and Bettger, but what they teach can be applied to management, marketing and everything else. Sales is at the heart of any commercial corporation. . . . But have you read Drucker?

TED

(*Shakes his head*) I always saw that as the Cult of Management.

                    DICKIE
No, Drucker's terrific. You've got to read him. Here . . .

Dickie looks for his attache case, pulls it up, opens it and takes out a slender brown-jacketed volume – The Effective Executive *by Peter Drucker.*

                    DICKIE
The insight packed into this little book is incredible.

He hands Ted the book, which Ted looks at.

                    TED
As soon as I'm back, I'll slip into Kroch's and pick up a copy.

                    DICKIE
No, keep it – I've practically memorized it and it's much easier for me to go to Kroch's when I get back. . . .

                    TED
Thanks.

Ted looks down at the book again.

Fade to black.

EXT./INT. INTERNATIONAL TERMINAL, AIRPORT – DAY

Some days later Ted arrives at the air terminal with executive-style carry-on luggage, accompanied by Fred with a patch on his right eye and crutches.

                    TED
(Very upbeat) . . . But you've got to admit it looks like you're well on the way to a complete and total recovery. I mean, it's incredible.

Fred stops.

                    FRED
Just cut the Pollyanna-Little-Miss-Mary-Sunshine "complete recovery" crap. My God, you're almost pathological! Sometimes I'd like to wring your neck.

TED

Well, the mood swings are new.

INT. BARCELONA AIRPORT CAFÉ – DAY

Fred in uniform, a black patch over his right eye, standing on crutches leaning against the bar having coffee with Ted, whose all-in-one suit bag is on the floor next to him.

FRED

Rehabilitation is fine for houses. But for people it's – unspeakably boring. Do you know what the whole basis for physical therapy is? Doing the same thing, over and over again.

With his arm, Fred indicates an unspeakably boring repetitive movement.

FRED

(*To waiter*) Una paja, por favor.

TED

But it's really important.

FRED

Oh, yeah.

Fred leans over, puts the straw in his cup of café-con-leche and takes a long pull.

FRED

But where's the upside? Learning how to do things you already knew how to do much better before.

TED

You really should read Drucker.

FRED

You think it's applicable to the navy?

TED

Yeah – and to whatever you do afterwards. . . .

Fred, pensive, takes another pull on his coffee.

FRED

I've started remembering things about that girl you talked about. Marta.

As if his injuries have weakened Fred's emotional self-control, his voice becomes tremulous.

FRED

Everything's gone so badly. . . . I'm not going to be a crybaby about this.

INT. AIRPORT DEPARTURE GATE — DAY

On the PA system the TWA flight to New York is announced, first in Spanish and then in airport English. At the barrier of metal detectors, where passengers and visitors separate, Fred waits slumped over his crutches as Ted prepares to embark. Fred is a somewhat sad spectacle now; just before Ted's departure, Fred signals him and Ted dutifully walks over to him.

FRED

I remember something about a limbo stick.

TED

Yeah, there was a limbo stick.

EXT. AIRPORT TARMAC BUS — DAY

One of the elongated trailer-buses pulls away from the terminal, taking passengers to the TWA plane parked in the distance. From inside the terminal Fred, hunched over his crutches, watches the trailer-bus head out toward the plane.

EXT. SOMEWHERE IN THE MEDITERRANEAN — DAY

The Sixth Fleet sailing full speed ahead.

EXT. BARCELONA AVENUE — DAY

Trade-fair girls on motorcycles, possibly including Aurora or others, racing up Paseo de Gracia.

132

INT. TED'S BARCELONA OFFICE (IHSMOCO) — DAY

Fred, who in Ted's absence has appropriated his office, sits with Greta in front of a mockup of Port Call Confidential's *long-postponed Barcelona edition carrying the one-word headline: LIBERTY! Aurora is just coming in the door with a large envelope under her arm. Nuria works in the background.*

GRETA

Why shouldn't I draw angels and demons?

FRED

Well . . . it's kind of strange.

AURORA

Hola!

FRED & GRETA

Hola!

From the big envelope Aurora slips out an original black-and-white drawing in Greta's style showing the fleet arriving at Barcelona, along with three different-sized stat reductions of the same image.

FRED

Thanks. (*Looking at the art.*) Great. (*To Greta.*) That's really nice. Thanks. . . .

Nuria joins Fred in looking at the drawing. Greta starts reading from the paper's text. Aurora looks over her shoulder.

GRETA

These tours sound interesting.

AURORA

Here's something about the trade fair. . . . (*Reading photo caption.*) "Colorful outfits identify the Trade Fair's *azafatas,* whose efficiency and charm are world-renowned." (*Re: picture.*) It's Montserrat.

Greta looks at the article and picture.

FRED

(*Leaning close to the drawing*) Uh, Greta, what are these figures here?

133

Greta leans over and takes a look.

> FRED

. . . hovering over the flight deck . . . ? Are those wings?

> GRETA

Yes.

> FRED

What are they supposed to be doing there?

> GRETA

They're hovering.

> FRED

(*Upset*) Well, what are they doing hovering there?

> GRETA

I suppose they're watching over everything.

Fred grabs the smallest of the three stats of the drawing and looks at it closely.

> FRED

I'll just say you don't know much about helicopters.

> GRETA

(*Looking around*) So this is where Ted works.

Getting up to go, Greta puts on a smart cap.

> FRED

Yes. This is the shrine.

FALL BARCELONA/CHICAGO AIR TRAVEL MONTAGE

Montage images – Correfoc: fireworks-spewing dragons chasing young people in Barcelona's streets, including Fred, Greta, Aurora, Montserrat and JAVIER *(the brother of one of the girls); Ted at airport near TWA or British Airways counter; Greta waving to Ted at airport cafeteria; Ted, Dickie Taylor, and a woman IHSMOCO executive standing in diagonal file with extremely sad expressions, holding back tears, trying to smile at some humorous remark Jack (seen if at all as a shadowy half-profile near the camera) has made; beautiful panoramic view of Barcelona.*

TED *(v.o.)*

Commuting between Barcelona and Chicago that fall, I started routing the trip through London to be able to fly into Chicago directly, avoiding New York and Madrid entirely. Twice I ran into Greta on the London leg – apparently she was visiting friends there.

It was incredibly sad watching Jack's decline, but he still had good days and the memory of these will always be incredibly important for all of us. Chicago and Barcelona had never seemed more beautiful than they did that fall.

EXT. AIRPORT, STREET ADJACENT INTERNATIONAL TERMINAL – DAY

Fred picking Ted up at airport in Ted's car.

EXT./INT. HIGHWAY, TED'S CAR – DAY

First exterior of car on the highway driving in from the airport, then inside the car with Fred driving and Ted the passenger. Fred wears sports clothes and Ted a suit.

FRED

(Upset) You didn't say anything about getting married.

INT. HIGHWAY, TED'S CAR – DAY

FRED

(Querulous verging on indignant) You think marriage is going to solve all life's problems. . . .

TED

Well, a lot of them.

FRED

I've never seen you like this – so cocky.

Ted grins and looks cocky.

135

FRED

Aren't you taking a lot of things for granted? The boyfriend's
still in the picture.

TED

(*Seriously*) I'm not taking anything for granted. Until we've
actually exchanged vows –

FRED

– That's it. You think wedding vows are going to change
everything. Your naivete's astounding.

Fred looks in Ted's direction as if to take a closer look at all the naivete.

FRED

Didn't you ever see *The Graduate?*

TED

You remember *The Graduate?*

FRED

(*Annoyed*) Yeah, I remember some things. (*Pause.*) Apparently
you don't . . . The end?

Ted thinks.

FRED

Katharine Ross has just *married* this really cool guy – tall,
blond, very popular, the "make-out king" of his fraternity at
Berkeley – when this obnoxious Dustin Hoffman character
shows up and starts pounding on the glass at the back of the
church, acting like a total asshole. (*Fred does his version of the
Dustin Hoffman wail.*)
    Does Katharine Ross tell Dustin Hoffman, "Get lost, creep.
I'm a married woman!" No – she runs off with him, on a bus.

Ted is stunned.

FRED

That's the reality.

TED

Thanks a lot.

EXT. PICTURESQUE BARCELONA LOCATION – DAY

Ted and Fred standing and talking at some scenic Barcelona spot such as the Plaza del Pi, Rambla Catalunya, the Quay de la Fusta, or Montjuich with the port area panorama below.

TED *(v.o.)*

Then Fred's tone changed completely and he became almost insanely positive about the approaching wedding.

FRED

(Very happy) Of course I like her. She's great. The thing is, you're really right for each other – it makes sense. *(Pause for thought.)* She's accepted and everything?

TED

Of course she's accepted.

FRED

That's great then.

TED *(v.o.)*

Initially I ascribed the change to the sometimes highly emotional mood swings Fred had been experiencing since the shooting.

EXT. PARK GUELL – DAY

A long shot of Ted and Montserrat walking together in the middle of a beautiful park in the late afternoon. They are talking but we can't hear what they say. It should look poignant and romantic. Montserrat kisses Ted. She might or might not be crying a little bit.

EXT. GOTHIC QUARTER – DAY

The morning of another day. In the small plaza between the old cathedral and the Church of San Severo – one wall of which is decorated with pictures in ceramic tile of scenes from the war against Napoleon – wait Ted in a blue suit and Fred and Frank in uniform.

TED

Positive thinking is fine in theory, but whenever I try it on a systematic basis, I end up really depressed.

FRED

It hasn't really worked for me, either.

He indicates his eye-patch.

FRED

(*Sees something*) Oh, God.

The Consul can be seen walking toward them from the other end of the pedestrian street.

TED

Oh, good.

FRED

"Oh, good"? You invited that guy?

TED

He was great when you were in the hospital – I think you might have misjudged him. He seems like a nice guy.

FRED

He's paid to act that way.

As the Consul arrives he, Ted and Frank exchange "hellos" and "good mornings." Fred holds back, sulking and barely civil.

FRED

(*Looking around*) There's no one from the bride's side.

They look around. There are a couple of derelicts and obvious tourists, but no likely candidates for the bride's party.

TED

Her parents wanted to keep it really small.

FRED

They must be *delighted* having their daughter marry an Estadouni-DENSE.

TED

No, they're not that way. Her family's terrific.

They stand around. No one comes. Meanwhile, the Old Quarter quiet is broken by a teenager riding by on a noisy and ridiculous quasi-antique motorbike. He suddenly comes to a stop in front of them, hops off and rests the bike on its stand.

TED

Javier!

JAVIER

(*Very friendly*) Hola, que tal.

He quickly takes out a note and starts to read from it in a sort of English. His English should be excruciatingly bad but he insists on persisting with it. He stares at one or more of the English words on the paper in disbelief.

JAVIER

My father wanted me to explain you: "Sorry for the inconvenience. . . . Please take coffee – we there be soon."

FRED

Everything's fine with your sister?

JAVIER

Yes. Everything – fine. We do not understand where she is, but – not a problem.

FRED

Oh, God.

JAVIER

No, not a problem. My sister is not a flah-kay –

FRED

A . . . "flake"?

JAVIER

No. She is a very serious girl – (*To Ted.*) Do you know that?

TED

Yes.

EXT. PLAZA SAN JAIME – DAY

Ted, Fred, the Consul, Frank and Javier turning the corner into Plaza San Jaime. They cross in front of the Palace of the Generalitat, where a phalanx of "Mossos de Squadra" in dress uniform has assembled for a foreign dignitary's visit. Behind them are some mounted municipal police.

CONSUL

I could swear this car was following me all morning.

TED

What did it look like?

CONSUL

It was a . . . blue Citroen.

TED

Did you notice the plates?

CONSUL

It had Gerona plates.

Fred and Ted stop and exchange serious looks. They look around.

TED

(*To the Consul:*) Before he was shot Fred was tailed by a French-make car with Gerona plates – but I can't believe they'd be that stupid.

FRED

No. Standards in everything are declining – terrorists aren't immune to that. Just because they occasionally succeed in killing or maiming one of us – (*he indicates his eye-patch*) – doesn't mean they're not a bunch of cretins. We know they're sexually impotent.

INT. MESON DE CAFÉ – DAY

Standing at the bar of the little café they all order café "cortados" except Fred.

140

TED

Things have been pretty tense. I've hardly slept in a week. Her old boyfriend resurfaced on Wednesday.

JAVIER

Not a problem.

FRED

(*To barman*) Una . . . cuba libre.

CONSUL

(*Principally to Fred:*) I don't think "anti-Americanism" is really that significant a phenomenon – it's certainly nothing to take personally.

FRED

Sorry if I take it personally.

Indicates his eye-patch again.

TED

What is it, then?

CONSUL

This is how I see it. Well – let me use an analogy: The United States is like an . . . enormous ant farm –

FRED & TED

– Oh no! Not ants!

Fred and Ted respond with some mirth, but the Consul continues without pause.

CONSUL

(*For Javier's benefit*) An ant farm is a see-through plastic case enclosing an ant colony. It's sold as a toy for children who can watch the ants build their own little society inside.

With his hands the Consul indicates the approximate shape of an ant farm. Javier nods.

CONSUL

(*For the group*) I think the U.S. is sort of the ant farm for the rest of the world. But people in other countries can't observe

141

the ant farm directly. They must rely on journalists and commentators for a description of everything going on there. The problem is that these people all seem to, uh, hate ants.

They all seem quite impressed with this explanation, including Fred.

EXT. STREET OUTSIDE CAFÉ – DAY

Shortly afterward they all leave the café in high spirits – the Consul has taken on the life-of-the-party role. He, Fred and Frank are walking together.

> CONSUL
> You know, I'm not sure if anyone's ever mentioned this to you, but it looks to me like you could be shaving in the wrong direction.

> FRED
> I wonder about that all the time.

> CONSUL
> Your father never taught you?

> FRED
> You know, he uses an electric razor and it never occurred to me to ask him.

> TED
> (*Surprised*) Your father uses an electric razor? I never knew that.

> FRED
> Well, he's light-haired, so it never really mattered. But I really have to shave. It's no joke. (*To Consul, with great interest.*) What is the right way to shave, then?

> CONSUL
> Well, first you –

They disappear around a corner.

EXT. PLAZA ADJ. CHURCH – DAY

Now a few other people wait with them in the small square adjacent the church. Javier walks toward Ted with a big smile on his face.

JAVIER

They have just explained me – all are coming now. Not a problem.

Javier clasps Ted's hand in solidarity; Ted tries to look less worried. As Javier goes back to be lookout, Fred comes up and speaks to Ted in a confidential, serious tone.

FRED

(*Speaking incredibly quickly, in a low voice*) Listen, I know this is awkward, but you're going to be leaving town and, now that everything seems set, I wanted to mention . . . I'm going to be calling Montserrat to ask her out. I can't yet remember everything about how it was before I was, uh, shot, but since then I've had this incredible feeling for her that I've never had before. It's not some silly crush; I've seen her in all sorts of situations and contexts, some really, really difficult – I mean, you clearly realized the way things were before she did, and it was very hard for her, as it had been hard for you before. We've talked for hours on the phone and she's so charming and fascinating I can't bear the thought of going back without her and I'm sure she'd like San Francisco much better than Chicago and it would be great going to the Lake summers with you and Greta there.

While talking they can see Montserrat approach with Ramon as her escort. But she seems encouragingly aloof from him.

TED

Oh, God. . . . You always do this.

FRED

I always do this?! Could you just try to be a little sympathetic?! A little cousinly?! . . . – Pretend I'm one of your customers.

TED

Okay, but, Jesus, do you have to get into all this now? Things are a little tense. I'm getting married and the bride hasn't shown up.

FRED

She'll show up. She's ga-ga for you.

TED

You think so?

FRED

I don't think she spent all that time at the hospital just to see how *War and Peace* turned out. . . .

TED

Greta's actually looking forward to the eighty channels of television and abundance of consumer products in the U.S. I mean, it doesn't bother her at all.

FRED

Of course not. . . . She's terrific. . . . (*Intently.*) You more than anyone should want Montserrat to have some chance for happiness in life.

TED

You're Montserrat's chance for happiness in life?

FRED

(*Offended*) Maybe.

TED

What's your plan – you're going to play it somewhat cool?

FRED

I'm going to play it really cool. . . .

They stop talking as Montserrat and Ramon draw closer; Montserrat greets Ted and Ramon actually approaches Fred.

RAMON

I know some people think articles I wrote in some way related to your shooting. I don't agree that a journalist should be criticised for writing articles he believes to be true. But if anything I have done caused you harm in any way, please accept my sincere regret. If there is anything I can do for you in the future, please do not hesitate.

FRED

Thank you very much. . . . Actually, I think there might be something.

Two cars arrive as close to the church as they can get. The doors open and the bride's family gets out, then her father and Greta herself, who's wearing a nifty white suit-dress. Everyone except the bride's immediate party walks quickly back toward the church. Frank walks with the Consul, who, turning into the small street, sees the blue Citroen with Gerona license plates that he thought had been following him.

CONSUL

That's the car I thought was following me. It turns out they were just coming here too.

Two dark young men emerge from the courtyard of a gothic palace and follow them as they walk, light windbreakers wrapped around their hands.

JAVIER

(*Sounding the alarm*) Hey!

Frank – turning to see the two men starting to pull the cloth off their pistol-hands – reflexively lunges, trying to protectively knock the Consul down. The gunmen, who have raised their pistols to fire, shoot badly in the confusion, then break and run down an alley. Fred, Ted and Frank – holding his arm where it was grazed by a bullet – run after them. Behind all is chaos. The blue Citroen swerves out near the gunmen, a door swings open and they try to get in running alongside, but the car's inexpert driver piles it into a narrow alley wall. He lunges out and starts running with the other fugitives.

One gunman abruptly stops in a doorway and puts a fresh clip in his semi-automatic and turns it on the pursuers. It suddenly dawns on the three that, weaponless, they are pursuing armed assassins. They reverse direction and run as the gunman fires a few times wildly and then continues running himself. From cover the three watch as the assassins run into the Plaza San Jaime, where a brigade of heavily armed

145

Mossos de Squadra police was previously shown assembled for a state visit.

MOSSOS COMMANDER *(o. s.)*
(*In Catalan*) Halt! Drop your weapons! Hands in the air!

From the square comes the distant sound of weapons being dropped and police formations quick-marching. One column of Mossos can obliquely be seen marching at a trot to seal off the visible side of the plaza.

TED
You're right. Standards in terrorism have declined.

Fred nods.

FRED
(*To Frank:*) Are you okay?

FRANK
Yeah. It's nothing.

EXT. PLAZA – DAY

Turning back to the small plaza near the church, they see a crowd of people standing and kneeling beside a person who lies bleeding on the pavement. They start running back.

FRED
Jesus – the Consul.

They run toward him as a hospital ambulance-van and other police and official vehicles arrive with sirens blaring. Beyond where the Consul lies seriously bleeding on the pavement, Ramon sits stunned, holding his bleeding arm, attended by one or two people.

EXT./INT. AMBULANCE VAN – DAY

Fred accompanies the now-bandaged Consul, Ramon and Frank in the back of the van with a medic as it races to the hospital. The Consul lies in a stretcher bed with IV units, looking somewhat relaxed with his arm behind his head. The others are bandaged and sitting. The medic is taking Ramon's pulse or plugging an IV unit into his arm.

FRED

No, the hospital's great – you'll love it. People read to you. I was thinking Admiral Mahan's *The Importance of Sea Power in History* might be good – have any of you read that?

They all shake their heads "no."

FRED

No, you're going to have a great time. . . . And the physical therapists at this hospital are – terrific.

RAMON

They are beautiful?

FRED

(*Puzzled*) Well . . . maybe "Inner Beauty." . . . They're these two, big Basque guys – on the homely side, actually. But "Inner Beauty." Yeah.

Ramon nods and looks away.

INT. HOSPITAL – DAY

A large hospital room with the Consul and Ramon in beds and Frank in a chair. Fred has been reading from Admiral Mahan's book but conversation has broken out.

RAMON

What makes you so certain that the attack of yesterday was not planned by the covert agencies of the United States – or known to them beforehand and allowed to happen?

Fred looks at Ramon a moment, then goes back to reading aloud from Mahan.

FRED

"The weapons with which Suffren fought are obsolete; but the results wrought by his tenacity and fertility in resources are among the undying lessons of history . . . "

EXT. A BEAUTIFUL LAKE — DAY/SUNSET

A beautiful lake with a few rustic cottages and much green foliage around it, at sunset, twilight time.

TITLE: *superimposed:* The Lake.

EXT. VERANDA, LAKESHORE COTTAGE — DAY/SUNSET

Fred and Ted in summer clothes on a terrace stand talking near a charcoal grill where hamburgers and hot dogs are cooking.

                    FRED
My idea was to anchor in the middle of the lake and fish from there. – Anything I caught I would have split with you. – So I put that big mooring stone in and started paddling out. It rode really low in the water, sort of cool, like the HMS *Hood* on its way to the Battle of Jutland –

                    TED
– the *Hood* wasn't at Jutland –

                    FRED
– but, maneuvering for a turn, I made a serious misjudgment; (*reenacts, leaning to one side while paddling*) suddenly I felt something very cold on my trouser-seat . . . and, like the *Hood,* it went right down.

                    TED
Thank God you were a good swimmer.

                    FRED
Yeah. Phew.

Meanwhile Montserrat and Greta have come out with a tray of hot dog and hamburger buns and condiments. They are in a very good mood.

                    GRETA
Look.

Greta holds the long hot dog buns over the long hot dogs, and then the round hamburger buns over the round hamburgers.

148

GRETA

These go with these, and these with those.

Both are delighted. Ted and Fred look at the buns with a new respect. Ted puts them down to toast, and takes off some already-toasted hamburger buns and grilled burgers. Montserrat is served the first burger with Heinz ketchup. She takes a large bite of it warily. Her expression makes clear she has just tasted her first ideal-burger.

TED

You see. We're not such idiots.

Greta starts her burger, with similar results.

AURORA (*o.s.*)

Hola, Tayd!

They all look left. Aurora, wearing tennis whites, enters from the left, followed by Dickie, also wearing whites.

AURORA

Mmmm. . . . Va muy bien con pan con tomate, sabes?

MONTSERRAT

Si?

The three women go inside. Fred, Ted and Dickie watch them.

DICKIE

She's really beautiful.

TED

Yeah.

FRED

I'm not sure how important that is.

DICKIE

No, I really like her. There's just this one thing: She keeps asking me about my "underwear" – and then smirking – as if I'm supposed to know what she's talking about. . . . What are "weekends of fun"?

Fred, surprised, looks at Ted. Ted doesn't seem very surprised.

149

                              TED

Oh, that. Montserrat was the same way. Apparently it's some
Barcelona girl thing.

                              FRED

It does sound familiar.

                             DICKIE

Hunh. Odd.

                              TED

You see, that's one of the great things about getting involved
with someone from another country – you can't take it
personally. What's really terrific is that when *we* act in ways
which might objectively be considered incredibly obnoxious or
annoying, –

Fred and Dickie nod.

                              TED

– they don't get upset at all, they don't take it personally, they
just assume it's some national characteristic.

                              FRED

"Cosa de gringos."

                              TED

Yeah.

                             DICKIE

Fantastic.

                          TED & FRED

Yeah.

*They stand on the lodge terrace with thoughtful expressions, pensively
sipping their beers, nodding in agreement, looking out toward the Lake.
Inside someone puts on music.*

Fade to black.

CREDITS – MUSIC – "BEAUTIFUL BARCELONA" MONTAGE

Metropolitan

Doomed   Bourgeois   In Love

Metropolitan had its first public showing at the Sundance Film Festival in Park City, Utah, in January 1990. It opened theatrically in Manhattan on August 3, 1990. The cast includes:

AUDREY ROUGET	Carolyn Farina
TOM TOWNSEND	Edward Clements
NICK SMITH	Christopher Eigeman
CHARLIE BLACK	Taylor Nichols
JANE CLARK	Allison Rutledge-Parisi
SALLY FOWLER	Dylan Hundley
CYNTHIA MCLEAN	Isabel Gillies
FRED NEFF	Bryan Leder
RICK VON SLONEKER	Will Kempe
SERENA SLOCUM	Elizabeth Thompson
Cinematographer	John Thomas
Costume Designer	Mary Jane Fort
Editor	Christopher Tellefsen
Music by	Mark Suozzo
With Original Music by	Tom Judson
Line Producer	Brian Greenbaum
Co-Producer	Peter Wentworth
Produced, Written and Directed by	Whit Stillman

Produced by Westerly Films in association with Allagash Films Ltd.
A New Line Cinema release

INT. CORRIDOR, ROUGET APARTMENT — NIGHT

*The corridor in a large prewar Park Avenue apartment, deserted,
bathed in a gold light. The door at the far end opens and* AUDREY
ROUGET *— wearing an unfastened evening dress, barefoot, her expression
distraught, on the verge of crying – runs down the corridor to her
bedroom. Her mother,* MRS. ROUGET, *follows at a calmer pace. Cut to:*

INT. AUDREY'S BEDROOM — NIGHT

*Audrey enters her room and, after momentarily glancing at herself in
profile in the mirror, throws herself on her bed, burying her face in the
crook of her elbow. Mrs. Rouget enters, walks around the end of the bed
and sits on the edge by Audrey. For a while she says nothing.*

> MRS. ROUGET
> You can't listen to what your younger brother says. (*No
> response.*) I can't think of anyone less an authority on female
> anatomy.

> AUDREY
> He can see. . . . It's enormous.

> MRS. ROUGET
> No, it isn't.

*Audrey brusquely gets up and looks at herself in the mirror to confirm
her own verdict.*

> AUDREY
> It's hideous.

> MRS. ROUGET
> I don't think you should take any more of those diet pills.

> AUDREY
> I'm not.

> MRS. ROUGET
> Well, you're being very subjective. You know, there was a
> survey of girls your age some years ago and nearly all of them
> were convinced that either their behinds, or their noses, were

grotesquely oversized. And there was no apparent correlation between this conviction and their (*gesture*) actual size.

AUDREY

Really? They did a survey of that?

MRS. ROUGET

Yes. . . . Why don't you show me the dress again.

Audrey stands and looks at herself in the mirror; she frowns. Mrs. Rouget examines the dress.

It is a bit full here, but otherwise it's lovely. Let me have it and I'll take it in right now.

AUDREY

(*Slipping out of dress, which her mother takes*)

Thanks, Mom.

Alone, Audrey continues examining herself critically in the mirror, particularly her "enormous" behind. Then she leans close to the mirror and slowly studies first one profile and then the other, trying to judge whether her nose might not be too big, too.

EXT. PANORAMIC VIEW OF MANHATTAN – NIGHT

Series of shots, from air or skyscrapers, shows Manhattan in December.

A superimposed title card reads: Manhattan – Christmas Vacation – Not So Long Ago.

Series of shots lowers to show the brightly lit Plaza Hotel and the Plaza itself. On the soundtrack a dance orchestra plays "Bye Bye Blackbird" and/or "Goodnight Ladies."

Young people in evening dress pour from the hotel in groups and pairs and crowd the sidewalk waiting for cabs – among them Audrey, NICK SMITH and JANE CLARKE. It is very cold out, making the wait for cabs seem worse. TOM TOWNSEND comes out of the hotel alone and makes his way through the mass to the corner of 59th Street. Waiting for the light, he looks back at the slick crowd. Meanwhile a cab pulls up in front of him, which Nick, followed by the others, makes a dash for; but Tom is there before them. Nick calls to him. In a long shot we see but do not

154

hear them talking; with a medium shot, their conversation becomes audible.

> TOM

Really, it's not my cab.

> NICK

We'll share it.

> TOM

But I don't want it.

> NICK

We'll share it – I insist. That way there'll be no ill-feeling.

> JANE
> (*Standing with Audrey beyond clear hearing range*) You're going to Sally's too?

> TOM

No.

> NICK

Well, that settles it. Come with us. That way we'll all be going in the same direction.

> JANE

You should come or we're going to freeze out here.

Tom gives up and heads toward the cab.

EXT MADISON AND PARK AVENUES – NIGHT

The cab races uptown, as music comes up and credits roll (if not put at front).

INT. FOWLER LIVING ROOM – NIGHT

Sally Fowler's afterparty is in progress. In the foreground CHARLIE BLACK *is seen in profile close-up talking to some person or persons o.s.; as the frame widens we see that his primary audience is the highly attractive* CYNTHIA MCLEAN, *although the group as a whole listens too.*

CHARLIE

Of course there's a God. We all basically know there is.

CYNTHIA

I know no such thing.

CHARLIE

Of course you do. When you think to yourself – and most of
our waking life is taken up thinking to ourselves – you must
have that feeling that your thoughts aren't entirely wasted, that
in some sense they are being heard. Rationally, they aren't;
you're entirely alone. Even the people to whom we are closest
can have no real idea of what is going on in our minds. But we
aren't devastated by loneliness because, at a hardly conscious
level, we don't accept that we're entirely alone.

I think this sensation of being silently listened to with total
comprehension – something you never find in real life –
represents our innate belief in a supreme being, some all-
comprehending intelligence.

*While Charlie speaks Nick, Jane, Audrey and Tom are entering by the
foyer door, visible from the living room.* SALLY FOWLER *approaches to
welcome them. Charlie doesn't pause in his analysis, though some of his
audience glance in their direction.*

CYNTHIA

That seems awfully subjective.

CYNTHIA

Of course it is. That's just my point. We all subjectively know
God exists. Then, usually in adolescence, we decide that that's
silly. Still later –

INT. SALLY FOWLER'S BEDROOM – NIGHT

*Audrey and Jane leave their overcoats on Sally's bed and are ready to
primp in her mirror.*

SALLY

What's his name again?

156

AUDREY

Tom Townsend.

JANE

No, I think it was something else.

AUDREY

No, it's Tom Townsend. I'm sure.

SALLY

He looks familiar.

AUDREY

(*Somewhat excitedly*) He's the guy who was sitting at the table behind ours, alone, without talking to anyone all evening. Then outside we all tried to get the same taxi, so Nick insisted he come with us.

INT. FOWLER LIVING ROOM – NIGHT

Charlie and Cynthia in discussion as before, with some others listening.

CYNTHIA

I don't see what that has to do with proving God exists.

CHARLIE

What it shows is that a kind of belief is innate in all of us. At some point most of us lose that, after which it can only be regained by a conscious act of faith.

CYNTHIA

And you've experienced that?

CHARLIE

No, I haven't. . . . I hope to someday.

EXT. FOWLER LIBRARY – NIGHT

Tom, socially inexpert, awkwardly tries to occupy himself looking at the Fowlers' bookshelves, while Sally finishes mixing a highball for him. In the background on the sofa FRED, *a gangly fellow somewhat older than the others (he is graduated from college), sleeps with his head back on the sofa backrest and mouth partly open.*

SALLY

I understand my friends tried to take your cab.

TOM

Actually it wasn't my cab. I was just there waiting for the light to change when it pulled up in front of me. I never take cabs.

SALLY

You never take cabs?

TOM

I either walk or take public transportation.

SALLY

Why?

TOM

A lot of reasons.

NICK

So you're one of these public transportation snobs. You look down on people who take taxi cabs.

TOM

No, not at all.

INT. FOWLER LIVING ROOM — NIGHT

The crowd is divided in at least two conversational groupings. In one, Charlie holds forth from a changed position, with a somewhat different listenership.

ESCORT I

. . . at least in the popular imagination.

CHARLIE

I don't think there is a popular imagination.

ESCORT I

What do you mean?

158

CHARLIE

Just that. I don't think there is a popular imagination.

Meanwhile, Jane, Tom and others (perhaps just Fred sleeping) are on the sofa. Audrey sits on a chair or footrest nearby, leaning forward to listen. Initially she has little to say, but her excited attention – like Audrey Hepburn in her early Gary Cooper -Maurice Chevalier Paris film Love in the Afternoon – *should make her the center of attention throughout it.*

TOM

Pomfret. Where did you go?

JANE

Farmington. Both of us (*indicating Audrey*) did.

TOM

Did you know Serena Slocum there?

JANE

The inevitable question.

TOM

What?

JANE

Guys always ask that. Serena had an incredible number of b.f.'s – boyfriends – at least twenty. She could manage it because they were all at different schools and she wrote letters incredibly quickly, three in a single study hall. She became really famous. It's incredible how naive some guys are. How did you know her?

Tom, stunned, says nothing.

AUDREY

That might give someone the wrong impression. She wrote a lot of guys, but I'm sure she liked some a lot more than others.

JANE

You think so? I never noticed that. (*To Tom:*) How do you know Serena?

159

TOM

I was one of her "b.f.'s."

JANE

Oh. . . . (*Embarrassed pause.*) Then you were "Pomfret." Your letters were good.

AUDREY

Yes.

TOM

What do you mean?

JANE

They were interesting. . . .

TOM

Serena let you read my letters?

JANE

No, she read them aloud.

TOM

I can't believe it.

AUDREY

She only read us letters which she thought were good – or really bad. But yours were good.

JANE

There was no suggestion of ridicule, if that's what's worrying you – at least not that I can recall.

AUDREY

I remember a long letter you wrote Serena about agrarian socialism. I think it was one of the first things to set Alice Dryer off about Marxism.

JANE

Since then she's joined the Underground Red Army. If she blows herself up, it'll be your fault.

AUDREY

It's actually surprising to see you at something like this. In your letters you expressed a vehement opposition to deb parties, and to "Conventional Society" in general. I take it you've changed your –

TOM

No, I'm just as much against them as I've ever been.

AUDREY

What made you decide to go tonight?

NICK

He got an invitation.

An embarrassed silence at Nick's rudeness.

TOM

He's right. I got an invitation and didn't particularly have anything else to do.

SALLY

I think that's the case with almost everybody.

JANE

No. Nick goes whether he's invited or not.

NICK

Unlike Tom, I'm in favor of these kinds of parties and want to show my support however I can.

CHARLIE

I don't know. It's a bit ridiculous for someone to say they're morally opposed to deb parties and then attend them anyway. It's untenable.

SALLY

Everyone does.

CHARLIE

That's no contradiction.

SALLY

I wasn't trying to.

TOM

I think it is justifiable to go once, to know at first hand what it is you oppose. I'd read Veblen, but it was amazing to see that these things still go on.

JANE

You're a Marxist?

TOM

No. I'm a committed socialist, but not a Marxist. (*Pause.*) I favor the socialist model developed by the nineteenth-century French social critic Fourier.

CHARLIE

You're a Fourierist.

TOM

Yes.

INT. HALLWAY, FOWLER APARTMENT − NIGHT

Tom, alone, looks at pictures in the hallway, taking his time. Slowly he moves back toward the sound of the afterparty, stopping to look at pictures along the way. Cha-cha music starts to come from the other room and then stops.

INT. LIBRARY, FOWLER APARTMENT − NIGHT

Nick, Cynthia, Sally, Charlie and Audrey. Fred sleeping.

CYNTHIA

But it's completely ridiculous.

NICK

The cha-cha is no more ridiculous than . . . life itself.

CYNTHIA

Well, it is ridiculous and, anyway, I don't know how to do it.

NICK

That can be remedied. (*Looks for record.*)

SALLY

You must have learned it in dancing school.

NICK

Cynthia was a dancing school dropout.

CYNTHIA

If I did, I've since forgotten it.

NICK

I don't think it's possible to forget the cha-cha (*the music starts – raising his voice*) – you must be blocking it out.

Nick starts refreshing Cynthia about the cha-cha. Tom returns to the room and watches with the others. Charlie and Sally start dancing with them. Fred looks up from his sleep with a startled expression and then closes his eyes again.

INT. FOWLER APARTMENT – NIGHT

Charlie and Tom stand talking next to bar.

CHARLIE

Fourierism was tried in the nineteenth century and failed. Wasn't Brook Farm Fourierist? It failed.

TOM

That's debatable.

CHARLIE

That Brook Farm failed?

TOM

That it ceased to exist, I'll grant you. Whether it was really a failure, I don't think can be definitively said.

CHARLIE

For me ceasing to exist is failure. That's pretty definitive.

163

TOM

Everyone ceases to exist. That doesn't mean everyone's a
failure.

INT. FOWLER LIBRARY — NIGHT

Audrey and Cynthia in intense discussion.

SALLY

You really feel that way?

AUDREY

I really do.

SALLY

Really?

AUDREY

Really.

INT. FOWLER LIVING ROOM — NIGHT

Nick, Tom and Charlie; Fred sleeping.

NICK

Your parents are divorced?

TOM

Yes.

NICK

Mine and Charlie's are, too —

CHARLIE

That's the exception, though; divorce is actually comparatively
rare among the standard New York social types — contrary to
what people might think.

NICK

Usually there's something wrong, though. Dead fathers are a
common problem. (*To Tom:*) Jane's father is dead.

TOM

That must have been awful for her.

NICK

Yes. It was tough on him, too.

CHARLIE

That's different, though; it doesn't mean a "broken home."

NICK

Well, it still means having your mother go out on dates.

CHARLIE

My point was just that the common image of divorce and decadent behavior being prevalent among New York social types is not really accurate; that's more Southampton.

NICK

The real canard is this idea that the children of happily married parents are saner and happier than we are. On the contrary, I think they tend to be really screwed up. Or else really boring – they have all these imaginary problems. Or both. . . . Take Fred (*indicates sleeping Fred*); his parents are a model couple, yet he's absolutely blotto. Drinking is his way of coping with all the happiness at home.

CHARLIE

He isn't drunk; he was just very tired.

INT. FOWLER PANTRY/KITCHEN — NIGHT

In half-lit pantry Tom, alone, gets himself a glass of water and drinks it, looking around at the enormous, immaculate kitchen. Audrey enters carrying some used glasses and an ashtray.

AUDREY

Hi.

TOM

Hi.

AUDREY

What are you doing here in the dark?

TOM

I was just getting a glass of water.

AUDREY

Oh.

*Puts glasses in the sink. A clock on the kitchen wall shows almost 6
a.m.*

It's gotten awfully late.

TOM

Yes. What time do afterparties end?

AUDREY

There's no . . . set time – they end whenever people go. Or
whenever the parents get up, though the last time I was here,
over Thanksgiving, Sally's parents asked us to stay for
breakfast.

TOM

That's amazing.

AUDREY

No one stayed – except Nick.

TOM

Really?

AUDREY

He likes everyone's parents.

TOM

I don't think I've ever met anyone's parents. Except Serena's –
once I had quite a long talk with her father.

AUDREY

What's . . . the situation between you and Serena now?

TOM

There is none.

AUDREY

When did you stop seeing each other?

TOM

Yale game weekend.

166

INT. FOWLER LIVING ROOM – DAWN

Light filters into the room. Only the hard core remains: Charlie, Tom, Audrey, Jane, Sally. Fred is awake but in a daze. Nick stands at the window, looking down at the avenue and at the adjacent buildings.

> NICK
>
> Dawn in the big city. There are eight million stories out there.

Pause. Nick continues to gaze out the window and then turns back toward the others.

INT. FOYER & ADJACENT WASHROOM, FOWLER APARTMENT – DAWN

Guys putting on overcoats – in Tom's case a torn light-colored raincoat with a zip-in lining.

WASHROOM

Tom enters washroom and opens his wallet: he has no folding money – in his pocket are some change and a subway token. He returns to the foyer. The girls come from the back of the apartment with their overcoats on. Everyone says goodbye to Sally at the door, with much cheek-kissing.

FOYER

> JANE
>
> You won't be going to any more dances?

> TOM
>
> No.

> SALLY
>
> That's a shame. Well, it was nice meeting you.

> TOM
>
> Thanks – it was nice meeting you.

Generic goodbyes on the elevator landing; the elevator arrives and everyone except Sally gets in.

NICK

(*Parodying Eurotrash*) Ciao, Sally. Ciao.

SALLY

Ciao. (*Calling out to Tom before the doors close.*) Good luck with your furrierism.

INT. ELEVATOR/LOBBY – NIGHT/DAWN

Rat Pack descending to lobby of Fowler building.

CHARLIE

Unless we get a Checker, we'll have to get two cabs.

TOM

Don't worry about me – I'm going to walk.

JANE

Really? But it's terribly cold.

TOM

I prefer to walk.

Elevator doors open on the lobby and they walk toward front.

AUDREY

You'll freeze dressed like that.

TOM

This is actually very warm – it has a lining.

Goodbyes, adieus, etc.

NICK

(*Again satirically*) Ciao, Tom, Ciao.

TOM

Goodbye.

INT. TAXI – DAWN/NIGHT

Jane, Nick and Audrey in back, Charlie in front.

AUDREY

He's going to freeze dressed like that in this weather.

168

NICK

Driver, follow that pedestrian.

DRIVER

Oh, Jeez.

EXT. PARK AVENUE – DAWN/NIGHT

Long shot of Tom walking up the avenue with taxi slowly trailing him. Preoccupied, he doesn't notice it.

NICK

Hey, fella!

Tom looks back at them.

JANE

We have a Checker – can't we give you a lift?

TOM

No thanks.

NICK

You sure?

TOM

Yup. Thanks anyway.

After waves and goodbyes, the taxi takes off. Tom starts across street (79th) continuing north. The cab stops at a red light. Tom hurriedly crosses avenue to the west, in advance of a crosstown bus.

INT. TAXI – DAWN

Nick is turned around watching Tom; Audrey also looks back.

NICK

He's getting a crosstown bus. That explains it. . . . A Westsider is among us.

Long shot of the light changing and the taxi pulling out.

Fade to black.

DAY TWO (Friday, December 20)

EXT. PANORAMIC VIEW OF MANHATTAN'S WEST SIDE — LATE
AFTERNOON

*Combination of pans and montage of old West Side, excluding most
recent landmarks.*

Title card: Manhattan's West Side

*Shots of West Side squalor and disrepair, then Tom's building, prewar
but unprepossessing, the entrance and lobby somewhat shabby. Cut to
shade-drawn window of Tom's room on drab interior courtyard.*

INT. TOWNSEND MAID'S ROOM (TOM'S ROOM) — DAY
(DARKENED)

*Prewar Manhattan "luxury" apartments typically had at least one tiny
"maid's room" bedroom with bath adjoining the kitchen. In the sixties
in less affluent families these were taken over by the sibling deemed not
to need a larger room, usually the eldest or youngest brother. Tom
occupied this room.*

*At 4 o'clock in the afternoon Tom is still deeply asleep in his narrow
maid's room bed. The camera examines some of the objects in his room.
Out for reading are a couple of the more interesting left-wing social
science classics.*

INT. BEDROOM OR LIVING ROOM AT SALLY S APARTMENT — DAY

*The room has a southwestern exposure, so the maximum amount of
daylight is still caught. Jane, Sally and Audrey, dressed casually but
with their hair set, in discussion.*

> JANE
> There is a real escort shortage. It's no joke.

> AUDREY
> (*To Sally:*) What was your impression of him?

> SALLY
> He seemed nice. I didn't talk to him much.

JANE

Do you think he's really forgotten about Serena? I doubt it.

AUDREY

He was pretty emphatic about it.

JANE

Too emphatic.

SALLY

He did seem a bit of a phony, going on and on about his opposition to deb parties just after attending one.

AUDREY

No, he explained that. He's against them in principle, but got the invitation and decided to go sort of as a lark, and because of his interest in Thorstein Veblen.

SALLY

Everyone's against deb parties in principle. But they don't go on and on about it.

JANE

I think he's sincere.

SALLY

I wasn't questioning his sincerity. I said I thought he seemed like a perfectly nice guy.

INT. KITCHEN, TOWNSEND APARTMENT – NIGHT

Clock says 5:10, but December darkness has already settled. Everything is quiet until the maid's room door opens and Tom steps out, still groggy, wearing a ragged outgrown wrapper over boxer shorts and an old shirt. He pours himself a bowl of cold cereal and sits down to read the newspaper while having it. Then he gets up, finds a pot of cold coffee, pours himself a cup, adds milk and sugar, and sits back down to the paper. MRS. TOWNSEND *enters the kitchen; she should seem quite nice – not a nag at all.*

MRS. TOWNSEND

Oh, good – you're up. Good morning – or should I say, good evening?

TOM

(*Not looking up*) Suit yourself.

MRS. TOWNSEND

I just wanted to remind you about returning your tuxedo.

No response.

Oh, so that's how it is.

TOM

(*Patiently, not unkindly*) Mom, I don't want to seem rude. I know I got up very late, but I'm having what, for me, is breakfast, and I really don't want to think about returning my tuxedo right now.

MRS. TOWNSEND

It's just that I think it's getting too late if –

TOM

Get off my back.

After this, hunches back over newspaper.

MRS. TOWNSEND

It's nearly six – they're going to close.

With concern, Tom looks at clock and is shocked by how late it is.

TOM

Oh, Jeezus!

He bolts up from his chair and back toward his room.

MONTAGE

Tom dressing in great hurry, putting tuxedo in box (saying to himself, in fear, "If I have to pay for another day. . . !"), rushing out of the apartment wearing raincoat (with lining), running along sidewalk, hurriedly buying subway tokens, waiting anxiously on subway platform, getting out of subway on other end, running up subway steps, running along sidewalk, arriving at the downstairs door of A.T. Harris, Formal Wear, and finding it closed. Tom shakes door and tries to get someone's attention inside. Finally, he gives up and, downcast, begins

172

walking homeward, repeating route but at slow tempo, looking at the cold cityscape, with sad music on soundtrack.

INT. TOWNSEND APARTMENT – NIGHT

Tom, still in a bleak mood, returns home with the evening clothes box under his arm. Mrs. Townsend is in the living room as he passes through.

MRS. TOWNSEND
(*Sympathetically*) They'd already closed?

Tom, looking down, nods his head affirmatively, as if too sad to talk about it easily. His surliness toward his mother has disappeared.

MRS. TOWNSEND
How much extra will it cost?

TOM
(*Voice nearly breaking*) Twenty-five dollars.

He starts to move on.

I'm sorry about what I said earlier.

MRS. TOWNSEND
Not at all. A girl called – her number's by the kitchen phone – she said it was a bit urgent.

INT. TOWNSEND KITCHEN – NIGHT

Tom talking on phone, Jane's voice on the other end.

TOM
Tonight?

JANE
I know it's very late, but we had trouble getting your number. Basically we'd all be going together, although officially you'd be Audrey's escort. . . .

Insert showing Jane on phone with Audrey sitting behind her, with a concerned look on her face.

. . . Audrey Rouget. . . . The party should be of some
sociological interest –

*Cut back to Tom, who stands facing the tuxedo box he left on the
kitchen table.*

– Peter Duchin, the St. Regis Roof, etc. Do you think you'd be
able to come?

Tom staring at tuxedo box.

TOM

Uuhhmm –

JANE

Actually, there's a bit of an escort shortage.

MONTAGE SEQUENCE

Tom, hurrying to dress, encounters wardrobe problems:

INT. TOWNSEND MAID'S ROOM – NIGHT

*Tom returns to his room with the cardboard tuxedo box, opens it and
lays the tuxedo out on his bed. From the chair where it's draped he picks
up the shirt he used the night before and, cautiously, sniffs one of the
armholes.*

INT. TOWNSEND MAID'S BATH – NIGHT

*Tom carefully finishes soaping one of the armholes and begins rinsing it,
using a towel to keep the rest of the shirt from getting wet. He picks up
the hair dryer and begins drying the wet areas.*

INT. TOWNSEND MAID'S ROOM – NIGHT

*Tom, in dressing fever, hunts to match two black socks, then opens
another drawer and finds only one pair of clean boxer undershorts – but
with the inseam ragged and so gone he could put his hand through it.
He looks somewhat defeated.*

INT. TOWNSEND MAID'S BATH — NIGHT

Tom gets out a roll of white adhesive tape and a pair of nail scissors.

INT. TOWNSEND MAID'S ROOM — NIGHT

On tabletop Tom lays out boxer shorts — pushing aside a copy of a book, Spengler's Decline of the West *— tapes up the opening as best he can, which is not very well.*

INT. TOWNSEND MAID'S BATH — NIGHT

Tom, now mostly dressed, takes bottle of Old Spice or other unfashionable aftershave or cologne and sprinkles it on his face and elsewhere, underarms, etc.

INT. PARSONS' COCKTAIL PARTY, LIVING ROOM — NIGHT

A pre-dance cocktail party in a large Park Avenue duplex apartment, the guests in evening clothes. Nick, Jane, Sally, Charlie and Cynthia are together at one end of the living room as RICK VON SLONEKER *and* SERENA SLOCUM *enter the other end like celebrities, with friends greeting them. Nick and others watch them enter.*

                    NICK
What a mystery — Serena and Rick Von Sloneker still together
— it seems like it's been months.

                    JANE
It has been months.

                    NICK
Well, one thing's certain: She's lost her virginity by now.

                    JANE
(*Exasperated*) How can you say that.

                    NICK
(*Pause*) You're right. Maybe she wasn't a virgin.

Von Sloneker sees them from afar and nods. Nick smiles and waves back with grotesquely exaggerated friendliness while audible only to SFRP [the Sally Fowler Rat Pack]:

Riff-raff!

SALLY

He's hardly that –

NICK

Oh, you mean because of his title, we're supposed to be impressed. On the contrary, the titled aristocracy are the scum of the earth.

JANE

How can you make a generalization like that?

NICK

Making generalizations is very easy – the problem is finding some facts to back them up.

JANE

And Rick's one of your facts.

NICK

He's a fact, unfortunately. He's not my fact.

INT. PARSONS' COCKTAIL PARTY, STAIRWAY AND FOYER – NIGHT

Audrey and Tom, with cocktail glasses, sitting on stairs talking. A couple of passersby say "hi" to Audrey, but she's too involved in the conversation to say more than a distracted "hi" back.

AUDREY

. . . *War and Peace* and, by Jane Austen, *Persuasion* and *Mansfield Park.*

TOM

Mansfield Park? You've got to be kidding.

AUDREY

No.

176

TOM

But it's a notoriously bad book. Even Lionel Trilling, one of
her greatest admirers, thought that.

AUDREY

If Lionel Trilling thought that, he's an idiot.

TOM

(*Incredulous*) Uh! The whole story revolves around – what – the
"immorality" of a group of young people putting on a play.

AUDREY

In the context of the novel it makes perfect sense.

TOM

Yeah, the context and nearly everything Jane Austen wrote
seems ridiculous from today's perspective.

AUDREY

Has it ever occurred to you that today, looked at from Jane
Austen's perspective, would look much worse than ridiculous?

EXT. PARK AVENUE NORTH OF COLONY CLUB – NIGHT

*SFRP members and some others in background leaving apartment
building and walking toward Colony Club. Everyone wears heavy coats
except Tom, again wearing the light-colored raincoat, with arms
hunched together for added warmth.*

JANE

(*To Tom:*) You must be freezing in that.

TOM

It has a lining.

NICK

What kind of lining is it? Are you going to wear a raincoat all
winter?

SALLY

Princeton's south of here – I guess it's a lot warmer.

TOM

No, I just didn't know where to get a good overcoat.

NICK

(*Incredulous*) Brooks, J. Press, Chipp, Tripler, Paul Stuart . . .

TOM

Actually, I haven't had the time to look.

INT. COLONY CLUB AND BALLROOM – NIGHT

Montage of shots showing people arriving at dance and dance in progress. [If direct filming impossible, use montage of still photographs concentrating on SFRP members at dance as if caught by Bachrach photographer.]

INT. BALLROOM – NIGHT

Tom talking with Audrey while leading her in an elementary, somewhat clumsy, back-and-forth step.

TOM

Isn't it a bit strange – going to school abroad?

AUDREY

Yes.

INT. BALLROOM – NIGHT

Partial view of table where Sally and Tom and Audrey sit across from an unidentified debonair young man, who offers them cigarettes from an unusually shaped box. Sally takes one and examines it admiringly. The conversation is in progress.

ESCORT I

(*Answering prior question, not shown*) English Ovals.

SALLY

(*Impressed, examining it*) It is oval.

TOM

(*Also looking at one*) From England.

Sally accepts and Audrey declines a light from the man's elegant cigarette lighter. Audrey cradles the cigarette in the palm of her hand, admiring it.

                              AUDREY
   It's beautiful.

INT. CORRIDOR – NIGHT

Serena, Von Sloneker and others are in a group talking. Tom, coming down the hall, sees Serena but conspicuously tries to avoid looking at her, as if he hadn't already. Serena turns toward him as he approaches – perhaps saying "hi" – but Tom walks by maintaining the pose that he hasn't seen her, which must seem unlikely to Serena. She watches him briefly, her aplomb apparently unscratched by the snub, then turns back to group.

INT. BALLROOM – NIGHT

Tom, Audrey, Fred, Sally and Escort 1 at a table. On soundtrack, orchestra, party sounds, and conversation of Escort 1 can be heard, but camera follows Tom looking at adjacent table in corner of the ballroom, where a delicately beautiful, very unhappy girl, on the verge of tears, talks with a stiff-faced young man, apparently her boyfriend. (On soundtrack Escort 1 is giving SFRP group – Audrey, Sally, Tom, Fred, etc. – his hangover remedy: "What you do is drink two highball glasses of water and take two aspirin before going to bed. Of course, before going out, it's good to drink a glass of milk to coat the stomach – whole milk, not skim – it slows the alcohol's absorption." *Fred:* "I thought absorbing alcohol was the whole point." *Escort 1:* "It works. I haven't had a hangover since fourth form year." *This dialog should be given no emphasis, just in background; focus of scene is what Tom sees at other table.) Meanwhile, the sad girl Tom is watching stops talking and waits for her companion's reply, which is sparing and hesitantly given. She continues talking, more upset, starts crying and stops talking. Tears roll down her face as she and her boyfriend remain silent. Tom turns away from them back to Audrey, who is now looking at the crying girl. She turns away and they exchange a serious-minded look.*

INT. BALLROOM DANCE FLOOR – NIGHT

Orchestra plays cha-cha music. Audrey teaching Tom how to dance the cha-cha, with him succeeding awkwardly.

INT. LIBRARY, FOWLER APARTMENT – NIGHT

At start of afterparty Jane talks with Tom confidentially; others are in the background.

> JANE
>
> You really shouldn't treat Serena that way.

> TOM
>
> What?

> JANE
>
> Giving her the silent treatment.

> TOM
>
> I'm not giving her the silent treatment.

> JANE
>
> Oh, come on.

> TOM
>
> I'm not giving her the silent treatment – I just don't have anything to say to her.

> JANE
>
> Listen, I know you're angry with her and you're probably right to be, but it's still not right to treat her that way. I think Serena really feels hurt by it.

> NICK
>
> (*Interrupts in his high-pitched incredulous-exasperated tone*) Oh-give-me-a-break! Serena Slocum?! A real feeling?!

> JANE
>
> Serena's basically a good person; she has feelings like anyone else.

> NICK
>
> I find that very hard to believe.

INT. FOWLER LIVING ROOM — NIGHT

SFRP and others assembled early in afterparty, Charlie holding forth again.

CHARLIE

All this is pretty deceptive.

NICK

All what?

CHARLIE

I think we're all in a sense doomed. Now everything seems great. We've gotten into competitive, some highly competitive, colleges, and things are going well; we're finally out of school; we're getting invited to all these parties – often by people we've never met before. Our adult life has just begun and already everything seems pretty terrific. And, best of all, this is just the beginning, with the presumption that things will just get better and better as they go on. On the contrary, I think we are all almost certainly doomed to failure.

NICK

What are you talking about?

CHARLIE

Downward social mobility. We hear a lot about the great social mobility in America, with the focus usually on the comparative ease of moving upwards. What's less discussed is how easy it is to go down. I think that's the direction we're all heading in. And I think the downward fall is going to be very fast, not just for us as individuals but the whole preppie class.

Charlie's listeners receive this with a momentary silence.

FRED

Where do you get all this?

CHARLIE

Just look around. Take those of our fathers who grew up very well off. Maybe their careers started out well enough. But just when their contemporaries really began accomplishing things, they started quitting, not openly, but in other ways – "rising

181

above" office politics; refusing to compete and risk open
failure; not doing the humdrum part of their jobs or only doing
the humdrum part; gradually spending more and more time on
something "more interesting" – conservation, civic concerns,
the arts – where even if they were total failures no one would
know it. Or else deciding they could really accomplish more
working on their own and starting their own company, which
is where the really big money can be lost.

NICK

Okay. I guess most of us know who you're talking about. I
can't deny your point. But unlike you, I always assumed I'd be
a failure anyway. That's why I've always planned to marry an
extremely rich woman.

Nick looks at Jane.

INT. LIBRARY, FOWLER APARTMENT – NIGHT

*Tom, getting something at the bar, talking with Audrey alone as party
continues in the other room.*

AUDREY

. . . pretty depressing.

TOM

A bit overstated, don't you think.

AUDREY

I'm not so sure.

TOM

"Doomed." Even if he were right, it wouldn't be any great
tragedy if some of these people lost their class prerogatives.

AUDREY

"These people" are everyone I know. (*Pause.*) Anyway, it's not
a question of losing "class prerogatives," whatever that means,
but the prospect of wasting your whole productive life, of
personal failure.

TOM

That's so melodramatic.

182

AUDREY

Life is melodramatic, if you look at all of it.

TOM

I don't know.

AUDREY

I think my father considers himself a failure, although I don't think he's one. Probably few people's lives match their own expectations.

INT. SALLY'S BATHROOM – NIGHT

Audrey touches up her makeup in front of the mirror. In background, Sally brushes her hair and drinks a glass of water, or gin or vodka.

SALLY

I always drink two glasses of water before going to bed anyway. It's great for your complexion.

INT. HALLWAY, FOWLER APARTMENT – NIGHT

Tom putting on his raincoat to go when Nick speaks to him.

NICK

I thought I should mention – I'm putting you on the floor committee for the Christmas Ball – essentially it just means you'll be able to go on your own – rather than as someone's escort – and that you'll get a white carnation for your lapel.

TOM

Thanks, but actually I wasn't planning to go to any more dances.

NICK

You weren't? Well, I strongly advise you to change your mind. . . . (*Confidentially.*) Is it that your resources are limited? This is about the only economical social life you'll find in New York. Music, drinks, entertainment, hot nutritious meals – all at no expense to you. Basically all you need is one suit of evening clothes – and a tailcoat. Dances are either white tie or black tie – so you only need two ties. (*Indicating Tom's tuxedo.*) You rented that from where?

TOM

A.T. Harris.

NICK

Good, you know about Harris. They also sell them, secondhand, very inexpensively. At Brooks you can get the wing collar and boiled shirt for the tails – they're not really expensive at all. But remember to get the little brass collar studs to attach the collar to the shirt.

TOM

Thanks a lot. My resources are limited, but it's not really that.

NICK

I know: You're opposed to these parties "on principle."

TOM

Yes.

NICK

Exactly what principle is that?

TOM

(*Pause*) Well –

NICK

(*Quickly, interrupting to tell him*) – The principle that one shouldn't be out eating hors d'oeuvre when you could be home worrying about the less fortunate.

TOM

Pretty much – yes.

NICK

(*The masterstroke*) Has it ever occurred to you that *you* are the less fortunate?

Silence.

I just mean there's something a tiny bit arrogant about people going around feeling sorry for other people they consider "less fortunate." Are the "more fortunate" really so terrific? Do you

184

want some much richer guy going around saying, "Poor Tom Townsend – doesn't even have a winter coat – I can't go to any more parties."

TOM

That's a bit cynical.

NICK

This is not just a matter of what you'd personally prefer. I'll tell you this in confidence – you've made a big impression on these girls –

TOM

(*Simultaneously*) – Oh, come on –

NICK

– No, they like you and are now counting on you as an escort.

TOM

I like them, too, but –

NICK

I'm not sure if you realize it, but they're at a very vulnerable point in their lives. All this is much more emotional and difficult for them than it is for us. They're on display. They've got to call guys up to invite them as escorts. And preppie girls mature socially much later than others do; for many of them this is the first serious social life they've had. If you just disappear now, they're going to take that as a personal rejection.

TOM

Give me a break.

NICK

I'm not entirely joking. I'm serious. You should come. If Thorstein Veblen were here (*indicates where Veblen would be standing*) he'd tell you the same thing. . . . [No passionate indictment of conventional Society would be complete without the material you could get serving on the floor committee of the Christmas Ball.]

I'll meet you at Brooks at four thirty – main floor, southwest corner where the pyjamas meet with the expensive shirts – across from the undershorts counter—the salesman is Oscar.

185

Nick hurries this last part as Audrey, looking particularly nice after a primping session in Sally's room, approaches them with her overcoat on; Tom is escorting her home.

EXT. PARK AVENUE — NIGHT

Tom and Audrey walking up the avenue.

> TOM
> As a romance, it never really existed.

> AUDREY
> Really?

> TOM
> I made a classic mistake. I fell for Serena long before I met her. I had seen her at a Chapin dance, but didn't really meet her until a year later. Even before we started going out, I had already built up a huge romantic vision about her. It should be just the reverse. You should get to know someone gradually, over time, before the possibility of falling in love even occurs to you, and possibly not even then.

> AUDREY
> So the experience has somewhat hardened you.

> TOM
> Yes. At least that it's a very bad idea to fall for someone if they don't for you.

> AUDREY
> Yes, but you can't know that you feel exactly the same way all the time. I suppose there will be some risk in any romance.

> TOM
> (*Unenthusiastic*) I suppose so.

Audrey stops under an awning.

> AUDREY
> This is my building.
>
> Thanks very much for coming.

Thank you.

AUDREY

You'll come tomorrow?—it'll be as a group again.

TOM

Yes.

Audrey turns back and gives Tom a small kiss, which accidentally lands on his lips. Tom then mildly reciprocates. Audrey is profoundly affected. They part immediately and Audrey darts in the door a doorman has materialized to open, with muffled "goodnights." Tom is left on the sidewalk.

INT. ROUGET APARTMENT – NIGHT

Audrey preparing for bed in a somewhat ecstatic frame of mind. In her bathroom, wearing a simple cotton nightgown, she drinks two glasses of water and then looks at herself in the mirror, putting her arms around each other. Only as an afterthought she leans forward and checks her profile. She does not look greatly displeased.

Fade to black.

DAY THREE

INT. TOWNSEND APARTMENT – DAY

Tom dressed in jacket and tie, about to go out. His mother is in the foyer, too, as he gets ready.

TOM

(*Picking up envelope*) Thanks, Mom – I know how tight things have been.

MRS. TOWNSEND

They haven't been *that* tight.

TOM

I'll pay you back next month . . . or in February.

Tom puts on his raincoat.

Has Dad called?

MRS. TOWNSEND

(*Critically*) He's never called here. You know that.

TOM

I thought maybe his office had.

MRS. TOWNSEND

No.

INT. ARTIFICIAL LIGHT, A.T. HARRIS FORMAL WEAR, RACKS AND
FITTING AREA

Tom stands in front of full-length mirror with SALESMAN/FITTER, *trying
tailcoat on.*

TOM

They're normally this long in the back?

SALESMAN

Yes.

TOM

Uhn-huhn . . .

*The salesman helps him slip off the tailcoat and put on an evening
jacket; Tom then looks at it in the mirror for a while.*

I think I'd prefer one more like the one I rented.

SALESMAN

This is the one you rented.

TOM

Oh. I didn't realize it looked like this. (*Pause.*) I guess it'll be
okay.

Nick and Tom leaving store after 5 p.m. and walking up Madison Avenue in conversation.

NICK

You haven't seen this? (*Stops and briefly unbuttons collar.*) Detachable collar – not many people wear them anymore. They look much better. So many things which were better in the past have been abandoned for supposed convenience.

TOM

I had no idea anyone wore those anymore.

NICK

It's a small thing, but symbolically important. Our parents' generation was never interested in keeping up standards. They wanted to "happy," but of course the last way to be "happy" is to make it your objective in life.

TOM

I wonder if our generation is any better than our parents'.

NICK

It's far worse. Our generation is probably the worst since . . . the Protestant Reformation. It's barbaric, but a barbarism even worse than the old-fashioned kind. Now barbarism is cloaked with all sorts of self-righteousness and moral superiority. . . . (*Pause.*)

TOM

You're obviously talking about a lot more than detachable collars. . . .

NICK

Yeah, I am. (*Pause.*) You're escorting Audrey tonight?

TOM

Yes. Well, really, we're all going as a group – technically I'll be her escort.

189

I like Audrey. She's getting pretty good-looking, too. Who would have expected it?

MONTAGE

Dances Week montage, unified by one song or musical theme on soundtrack (sound exclusively music):

Ballroom of dancers including SFRP members.

Nick, standing, talking debonairely with attractive girl.

Tom, sitting with Audrey in some nook, helping her touch up her makeup with a makeup brush from her purse.

Charlie expounding philosophically to a cluster of homely girls, who are very interested; Nick and another fellow approach the table and ask two to dance, Charlie the other; all get up.

Fred with his head down on one of the tables, apparently asleep, as one of the "old biddies" who organize the dances passes by, giving him a fierce look.

Nick, homely girls, and everyone dancing the Charleston.

As Serena Slocum and Rick Von Sloneker walk by, Tom's expression freezes; they provoke a different expression from each Rat Pack member.

Taxis racing uptown to a different (Jane Clarke's) building.

A crowd standing by the door as the cab with Jane in it pulls up and she gets out. Music fades. Nick to Jane: "They wouldn't let us in."

INT. JANE CLARKE'S APARTMENT — NIGHT

Jane's and Sally's places are similarly big, well-padded prewar apartments with slight differences in decor – the Clarke "library" has some books in it. Rat Pack assembled; early in each afterparty the cast should be slightly varied, which generally winds down to the same core group, with small changes, each night.

FRED
Why's he so successful with girls, then?

190

NICK

Rick Von Sloneker's tall, rich (*grudgingly*) good-looking,
stupid, conceited, dishonest, stupefyingly boring, a liar, bully,
drunk and thief, an egomaniac and probably psychotic – in
short, highly attractive to women.

CYNTHIA

You're completely unfair. You don't know anything about
Rick. He's not someone as comfortable in social situations as
you are. In fact, he's very shy –

Nick laughs caustically at this.

   – Rick is a considerate and sensitive man. The rest is just a
superficial game he plays – a facade – which you've obviously
been taken in by.

NICK

It's amazing the eagerness of girls like you to justify the worst
bastards imaginable as being sensitive and shy – acting like
total bastards is just a facade. But if any guy who really was shy
dared talk to you, you wouldn't give him the time of day – your
eyes would glaze over.

CYNTHIA

You're really hung up on Rick, aren't you? He must really
threaten you somehow.

NICK

That I might get VD from one of the St. Tim's girls he's been
out with.

*Cynthia, evidently taking this reference personally, slaps Nick hard
enough to hurt.*

   Please, don't do that again. For me it isn't erotic.

INT. CLARKE APARTMENT – NIGHT

*Tom looking intently out the window. Audrey kneels in the seat of the
armchair next to him.*

AUDREY

What are you looking at?

191

TOM

My father's apartment.

AUDREY

Where?

TOM

The seventh floor, corner apartment.

AUDREY

That's Kate Preston's building. Have your parents been divorced long?

TOM

The actual divorce was three years ago, but they were separated a year before that.

AUDREY

Do you see your father much?

TOM

We have lunch when I'm in town.

AUDREY

That's very little.

TOM

No, we have a very good relationship, probably much better than most people who see their father all the time. It's just that my stepmother's a writer, and having us around makes her nervous.
(*Silence.*)

AUDREY

I read that Lionel Trilling essay you mentioned. You really like Trilling?

TOM

Yes.

AUDREY

I think he's very strange. He says that "nobody" could like the heroine of *Mansfield Park*. I like her. Then he goes on and on about how "we" modern people, today, with "our" modern attitudes "bitterly resent" *Mansfield Park* because its heroine is virtuous. (*A puzzled look.*) What's wrong with a novel having a virtuous heroine? Finally, it turns out that he really likes *Mansfield Park,* so what's the point?

> TOM
> His point is that the novel's premise – that there's something immoral in a group of young people putting on a play – is simply absurd.

> AUDREY
> (*Challenging him*) You found Fanny Price unlikeable?

> TOM
> She sounds pretty unbearable, but I haven't read the book.

> AUDREY
> What?

> TOM
> You don't have to have read a book to have an opinion on it. I haven't read the Bible either.

> AUDREY
> What Jane Austen novels have you read?

> TOM
> None. I don't read novels. I prefer good literary criticism – that way you get both the novelists' ideas and the critics' thinking. With fiction I can never forget that none of it really happened – that it's all just made up by the author.

DAY FOUR

INT. UPPER EAST SIDE BEAUTY SALON – DAY

Jane, Audrey and Sally waxing their legs.

> AUDREY
> One thing I like about him is that he doesn't say all the expected things – he doesn't just agree with everything everyone else is saying.

JANE

That's true. He disagrees with everything everyone else says.
I'm not sure I prefer that.

The woman who is waxing Sally's legs pulls the wax.

SALLY

Ow!

INT. AUDREY'S ROOM OR BATHROOM — NIGHT

*Audrey in slip and underclothes looks at herself in the mirror. She
briefly examines her lower leg waxing job and then looks at herself
critically in the mirror, seemingly less unhappy about what she sees than
usual.*

INT. SWAN DINNER DANCE OR FOWLER LIVING ROOM — NIGHT

A ballroom dinner table made mostly of SFRPers.

CHARLIE

Do you know the French film, *The Discreet Charm of the
Bourgeoisie*? When I first heard the title, I thought, "finally
someone's going to tell the truth about the bourgeoisie." What
a disappointment! It would be hard to imagine a less fair or
accurate portrait.

SALLY

Of course: Buñuel's a surrealist – despising the bourgeoisie's
part of their credo.

NICK

Where do they get off?

CHARLIE

The truth is, the bourgeoisie does have a lot of charm.

NICK

Of course it does. The surrealists were just a lot of social
climbers.

194

INT. BALLROOM — NIGHT

Tom and Audrey dancing.

                    AUDREY
I like the French.

                    TOM
Really?

                    AUDREY
At least those I've met in Grenoble.

                    TOM
Actually, the only girl I know who studied in France stayed
over there and got married, so I guess she liked the French,
too.

                    AUDREY
I'm not sure I like them that much.

As they talk the music has ended and the dance floor started to clear,
when conga music starts. In the background a conga line has formed
and started to move, Nick at its head, with his long limbs making an
incongruous and intentionally ridiculous figure. Other SFRPers open
the line so that Audrey and Tom can join it. There is giddy excitement
and joy.

INT. BALLROOM CORRIDOR AND FOYER — NIGHT

Tom escorts Audrey to the outside door of the powder room.

                    TOM
What really goes on in there?

                    AUDREY
Oh, it's fabulous.

Audrey enters powder room. Tom waits outside, apparently in very good
spirits. Looking down at the carpet, a grin passes across his face.
Meanwhile, the super-preppie SAM ELLIOTT, *heading toward the men's*
room, stops to talk with Tom.

SAM

You seem to be in an awfully good mood, Townsend – of course you're in your element here.

TOM

Are you kidding?

SAM

(*Somewhat boozy and self-pitying*) You're part of it all, the whole Manhattan thing – it's different for those of us from the country.

TOM

You're from Greenwich.

SAM

North Greenwich.

TOM

This is your world – not mine.

SAM

Oh, come on! You're part of that Sally Fowler crowd – you can't get any more inside than that. Not that I particularly care; I don't believe in these things – (*noticing Serena*) – Oh, hi, Serena.

SERENA

Hi. (*To Tom:*) Hi, Tom.

Tom is silent.

SAM

How's Johnny?

SERENA

Fine. He's at the Holidays tonight.

SAM

Probably the big heart-throb there.

SERENA

(*To Tom:*) Tom, I think we should talk.

INT. CORRIDOR — NIGHT

Serena and Tom walking slowly and talking, Tom somber.

TOM

I haven't been giving you the "silent treatment." I just haven't been talking to you.

SERENA

Well, I've felt it.

INT. TERRACE — NIGHT

Serena leads Tom through big opened window onto a terrace overlooking Fifth Avenue. They walk to the edge.

SERENA

I love the St. Regis; it has all sorts of hidden nooks and crannies. It's really charming.

TOM

Yes. They'll probably knock it down soon.

INT. POWDER ROOM — NIGHT

Audrey primps in front of mirror. Pinches and pats her cheeks to put some red in them. [In earlier scene this should be recommended as a beauty technique.]

EXT. TERRACE — NIGHT

Tom and Serena talking.

TOM

I appreciate your telling me all this, but it hardly explains why you just left me there, waiting for you, without even a phone call to say that you weren't coming. I'm sorry it was such a bad time for you, but I don't see how that should make me feel any better.

SERENA

You don't? It always makes me feel better.

TOM

Well, it does make me feel somewhat better. But it doesn't really change anything.

SERENA

It shows that it wasn't intentional – to me that's an important distinction.

Tom, his face toward hers, thinks about this. Serena leans toward him and gives him a long kiss – for her the definitive end for an argument.

INT. BALLROOM CORRIDOR – NIGHT

Audrey walks along with a perplexed look, heading back to the ballroom, surprised that Tom hasn't waited for her. She passes where Tom and Serena went to get to the terrace.

EXT. TERRACE – NIGHT

Tom and Serena talking.

SERENA

No, it's definitely over with Rick. With some relationships, the breaking up is easier to understand than how you got involved in the first place. (*Pause – Serena seems exhausted.*) Do you think I'd have any trouble getting a cab now?

TOM

You're going already?

SERENA

I'm utterly exhausted – my mother's doctor's been giving me these vitamin shots, but they've worn off or something.

TOM

Shots?

SERENA

Vitamin B12 to keep my energy up.

INT. BALLROOM CORRIDOR — NIGHT

Serena, looking faint, stands with her overcoat near the elevators. Tom with his overcoat over his arm walks toward ballroom, encounters Fred going in the same direction and stops him.

TOM

Fred – something's come up and I've got to go out for a while. Could you tell Audrey that I should be back soon but that if there's any problem I'll meet her at Sally's.

Second thought – stops Fred again.

Should I not get back, could you see she gets there okay?

Fred, who looks poorly himself and holds the back of his hand against his mouth, shakes his head affirmatively to all Tom says.

Thanks a lot.

Fred nods again and continues hurriedly in the same direction he had been going; Tom turns back toward Serena. Camera follows Fred down the corridor to the men's room.

INT. BALLROOM MEN'S ROOM — NIGHT

Fred enters, seems about to puke in one of the washstands, but doesn't. The washroom attendant watches with concern.

FRED

Phew – thought I was going to puke.

Abruptly he gags and lunges for the washstand, where he does puke. The attendant, with a depressed, fatalistic cast to his bearing and expression, begins getting some paper towels.

EXT. STREET ADJACENT TO HOTEL ENTRANCE — NIGHT

A still sick-looking Fred leans over the curb with his hands on his knees while Nick stands on the street trying to flag down a cab.

FRED

. . . had hardly anything to drink. Must have been something I ate – those Vienna sausages . . .

INT. SLOCUM LIVING ROOM – NIGHT

Tom and Serena sit together on big sofa in semidarkness in the Slocums'
living room. A glass and a Coke bottle are on the coffee table in front of
Serena.

SERENA

Rick might project an image of masterfulness – older,
experienced, rich, successful with women – but you really
shouldn't feel in any way inferior to him.

TOM

I don't.

SERENA

You're actually far more mature than he is. Rick has some
really serious problems and is apparently not self-aware
enough, or maybe not bright enough, to ever do anything
about them. Beyond that, your idealism is something he
couldn't understand in a million years. (*Pause.*) Actually, I was
somewhat surprised to see you at the dances this week – you
used to be so opposed to that sort of thing.

TOM

I still am, basically. I went to the first one almost accidentally –
and that night just happened to fall in with an extraordinarily
nice group of people – otherwise, I wouldn't have gone to any
more.

SERENA

I'd hardly call Nick Smith "nice." He's a terrible snob.

TOM

But he's basically a nice guy, I think.

SERENA

His behavior toward Rick has been vicious.

TOM

What did he do?

SERENA

I don't know all the details – he tried to make a big stink about
some girl. Rick didn't want to talk about it. Apparently it was

200

awful. He thinks Nick could be really crazy – that for some reason Nick bitterly resents his popularity with girls.

TOM

That does jibe with something Cynthia was saying.

EXT. BOATS ON EAST RIVER – NIGHT

View as it might be from Gracie Square or Sutton Place.

INT. SLOCUM LIVING-ROOM – NIGHT

SERENA

I'm glad we finally had a chance to talk and clear things up.

Serena poses languidly, leaning back on sofa, her head resting on the back, her mouth slightly open.

TOM

Yes, it's a big relief to me, too. It was awkward having to give the silent treatment to the only person I actually knew.

Pause. Serena waiting to be kissed. Tom – very slow on the uptake – gradually leans forward and begins to kiss her.

INT. ST. REGIS LOBBY – NIGHT

Partygoers are leaving or milling about. Audrey, with her coat on and looking worried, stands with Charlie. Nick and other SFRP members are nearby.

AUDREY

I'm just worried that something's happened to him.

CHARLIE

I don't see how anything could "happen" to him in the hotel.

NICK

Maybe it was the same thing as Fred.

AUDREY

(*Worried*) Tom hasn't had much experience of places like this.

Maybe he went through one of those fire doors that lock from the inside and shut himself in the stairwell.

NICK

The fire stairs here aren't like that. I've had to use them to attend certain parties and have never had any problem.

AUDREY

I just don't understand where he could be.

INT. FOWLER AFTERPARTY, LIVING ROOM AND FOYER – NIGHT

Rat Pack sitting around in conversation, some walking in from other room. Audrey observes from the background, silent, her expression impassively unhappy.

CHARLIE

That's interesting. Actually there's very little social snobbery in the United States. It's not considered acceptable. There's almost a national taboo against it. It's looked down upon.

PREPPIE

That's good, isn't it.

CHARLIE

I'm not talking about what's good or bad – just making an observation of fact.

SALLY

Well, I think it is good. I can't stand snobbery or snobbish attitudes of any kind.

From the front door a faint but steady knocking can be heard. Sally finally notices it and calls to Nick, who's walking through the foyer with a freshened highball.

Could you see who's at the door.

With his free hand Nick yanks the door open. Tom enters.

TOM

Sorry to be so late.

202

Charlie and Audrey are stiff and cool at Tom's arrival; the others, too, are more reserved than usual.

JANE
(*From across room, in a loud voice*) Where were you?

TOM
Didn't Fred tell you?

CHARLIE
Tell us what?

NICK
The only thing we heard from Fred was – (*Makes puking motions and sounds.*)

SALLY
Fred left ages ago.

Audrey has gotten up to carry some things to the pantry.

TOM
Oh, God. I'm sorry.

AUDREY
Why?

TOM
I asked Fred to tell you –

AUDREY
Don't worry – it's nothing.

Her manner belies her words. Audrey continues out to the pantry, but leaving the door open.

JANE
Well, where were you?

INT. FOWLER PANTRY OR KITCHEN

A sad Audrey rinses glasses.

                              TOM

I had to take Serena home. She was feeling badly and was
going to go alone – she and Von Sloneker have broken up –
but it took longer than I expected. I asked Fred to tell you that
if I didn't get back in time, I'd meet you here.

                            CHARLIE

We didn't get that message.

                              NICK

We thought you had gotten trapped in the hotel somewhere.
Audrey was very concerned.

                              TOM

I'm very sorry.

                            CHARLIE

You sound very sorry.

                            CYNTHIA

I find it hard to believe that Serena broke up with Rick. It was
probably the other way around.

INT. SALLY FOWLER'S BEDROOM – NIGHT

*Audrey finishing buttoning her overcoat, her eyes reddish and
apparently on the verge of tears. She walks out of the room.*

INT. FOWLER KITCHEN – NIGHT

*Tom talking with Sally, trying to put his conduct in more favorable
light. Other SFRPers in background or coming and going in pantry.*

                              TOM

I'm worried about Audrey – she seems to have taken this so
hard. I'm a bit surprised. I had no idea Fred was going to get
sick.

                            CHARLIE

(*Coming in from pantry, overcoat under his arm*) Where do you
get off? You're "surprised"? At what? You were Audrey's

                              204

escort – yet you blithely left her stranded in the middle of the dance – then try to shirk the whole thing off on Fred.

TOM

I'm not trying to shirk it off on Fred. And I was not Audrey's escort – we were all there as a group. . . . In any case, I'm very sorry there was a mixup.

CHARLIE

There was no mixup.

TOM

It wasn't intentional.

CHARLIE

When you're an egoist, none of the harm you do is intentional.

INT. FOWLER FOYER – NIGHT

Tom entering the foyer from kitchen. Audrey is coming down the hall wearing her overcoat.

TOM

You're going already?

AUDREY

Yes. I'm really tired.

TOM

Just a second – I'll get my coat.

AUDREY

No, don't bother. Charlie said he'd take me.

TOM

I'd like to.

AUDREY

No, really, there's no need.

TOM

Listen, I'm really sorry about what happened tonight. I thought I'd be back much more quickly.

205

AUDREY

(*Voice belying words*) It's not important.

Jane and Charlie, with his overcoat on, come out from the kitchen.
Sally and other SFRPers are also around for the goodbyes.

EXT. PARK AVENUE IN 70S – PREDAWN DARK

Nick and Tom walking up avenue deserted except for those who would
be up at this time (with the winter solstice, this dawn is very late). For
a while the camera follows them walking in silence – Tom still subdued
from Charlie's rebuke. Their dress – Nick sports top hat and cane –
attracts notice from passersby.

NICK

I wouldn't let anything Charlie said bother you too much.

TOM

I've never thought of myself as a "bastard," an "egoist."

NICK

Listen – don't flatter yourself. Charlie's standard of polite
behavior is so exaggerated – at school he used to individually
answer all his junk mail.
    I like him a lot, but *don't* try to understand all his thought
processes. The summer I met him – we were ten – he was
trying to establish communications with the seagulls of
Easthampton. It was utterly hopeless – the Easthampton
seagulls are complete morons. We still spent several afternoons
approaching shorebirds saying, "We come in friendship."
They couldn't have cared less. Much like his efforts with girls
in recent years.

TOM

Oh, great: I'm hated by the preppie St. Francis.

NICK

I wouldn't worry about it.

TOM

(*Indicating building*) That's the building where my father lives –

206

NICK

Do you know Kate Preston?

TOM

No.

NICK

She lives there.

Walking by the service entrance, Nick notices a stack of boxes with some good-quality, though not new, toys on top.

NICK

(*Stopping to look more closely*) It's incredible the things some people throw out. Steiff stuffed animals. An Aurora model motoring set. A derringer. Do you remember the derringer craze? These are the toys of our generation. The childhood of our whole generation is represented here, and they're just throwing it out.

Tom is somberly silent during Nick's speech. They slowly move on, but then Nick stops again.

Maybe we should rescue the electric car set. It could really add to these afterparties.

They continue down the block. At the corner Tom stops.

TOM

I turn here.

NICK

See you tonight. And, listen – don't take this thing with Charlie too seriously.

TOM

No. See you tonight.

MONTAGE SEQUENCE

Tom walking down side street toward Madison Avenue, stopping and looking back before reaching the avenue and then heading south and going around the block to arrive again at the service entrance. He approaches the boxes slowly and gazes at them and the contents of the opened box for a long time, his expression maudlin. Finally he selects a toy derringer pistol and small Steiff stuffed animal and puts them in his pocket before moving on.

DAY FIVE

INT. ROUGET LIVING ROOM – DAY

Audrey, Jane and Sally in more casual preppie wear – yellow and green cashmere sweaters, corduroy pants, cotton turtlenecks. Audrey, typically, is a bit keyed-up – the others are calmer.

> AUDREY
> What I'd like to know is, is Tom basically a good person? If I were confident he were, it would be easier to know how to act.

> JANE
> That has absolutely nothing to do with it. He could be a perfectly nice guy, but that wouldn't keep him from acting like a total jerk if you don't act with some discretion.

> SALLY
> *(Absentmindedly, while examining herself in mirror)*
> Do you think he's Jewish?

> AUDREY
> *(Surprised)* Why do you say that?

> SALLY
> He's so intense.

> JANE
> Don't be a ninny. Townsend's hardly a Jewish name.

> SALLY
> Names don't mean anything. . . . You're probably right, though.

AUDREY

My feeling is that what happened last night had no real significance. It was just bad luck that Fred got sick.

JANE

I can't believe you're talking this way. He totally humiliated you last night.

AUDREY

Whether I've been humiliated or not is something I can judge for myself, and I don't think Tom's that way.

JANE

I'm not sure you can judge for yourself. (*Pause.*) Be careful, Audrey. . . . There's something dubious about Tom.

AUDREY

What?

JANE

This whole thing about his being a "radical" when he's obviously not, and being "over Serena" when he's obviously not.

AUDREY

Everyone has some contradictions.

JANE

Anyone with as many conflicts as Tom, even if he seems nice, is better not to get involved with.

SALLY

By those standards, none of us should get involved with anyone.

JANE

You're probably right. But in this case, certainly.

AUDREY

(*After a pause, with some intensity*) Tom is the only guy I've really liked in my whole life. I'm not going to forget about him because of some apparent inconsistencies.

JANE

(*Pauses in amazement*) You hardly know him.

AUDREY

I know him very well.

JANE

You couldn't – you only just met him.

AUDREY

(*Determined, enigmatic*) Well, I do.

Jane looks baffled. A moment of silence.

INT. TOWNSEND APARTMENT – LATE AFTERNOON DARKNESS

*Clock shows time as 4:40 p.m. Tom, in shabby too-small wrapper and
eating a bowl of cold cereal, approaches living room desk where Mrs.
Townsend is addressing Christmas cards. Tom finishes swallowing large
mouthful of cereal before embarking on subject.*

TOM

When we moved, do you know what happened to my toys and
things?

MRS. TOWNSEND

They were put in storage.

TOM

Do you think some of them could have been sent to Dad's?

MRS. TOWNSEND

It's possible. Why? Do you need them? You're a bit old for
that sort of thing now.

TOM

No, I just had the feeling they went to Dad's.

MRS TOWNSEND

Why don't you call him, then?

TOM

I have. There's been no answer.

EXT. THE PLAZA — NIGHT

Long shot of some formally dressed young people crossing the Plaza during a snowstorm, trying to find taxis.

EXT./INT. HOTEL ENTRANCE AND ADJACENT SIDEWALK — NIGHT

SFRPers and others milling about at end of dance. Audrey and Tom stand together amidst others but not as if they were together as a couple. There is some distance and stiffness between them.

> AUDREY
> There's something about it snowing in the city, at night, with everyone dressed up, that reminds me of *War and Peace.*

> TOM
> Really?

> AUDREY
> Do you know what I mean?

> TOM
> Yeah, I think so. Though I haven't read it.

INT. FOWLER LIBRARY — NIGHT

Charlie mostly talking, others mostly listening.

> CHARLIE
> I don't think "preppie" is a very useful term. It might be descriptive for someone still in school or college, but it's ridiculous to have to refer to a man in his seventies – like Averell Harriman – as a "preppie." And none of the other terms people use – WASP, PLU et cetera – are much use, either. . . . That's why I prefer to use the term "UHB."

> NICK
> What?

CHARLIE

"UHB" – acronym for "urban haute bourgeoisie."

CYNTHIA

Is our language so impoverished that we have to use acronyms of French phrases to make ourselves understood?

CHARLIE

Yes.

NICK

"U – H – B" – the term's brilliant, and long overdue. But it's a bit of a mouthful. "U – H – B." Wouldn't it be better to pronounce it simply "uhb"?

CHARLIE

I didn't expect it to gain immediate acceptance.

NICK

No, I think it's a useful term – that it sounds ridiculous could be part of its appeal.

CYNTHIA

You see the world from such lofty heights that everything below seems a bit comical to you, doesn't it?

NICK

(*Stands up and looks down on her*) Yes.

CYNTHIA

You're so obnoxious.

INT. FOWLER LIBRARY/LIVING ROOM – NIGHT

Charlie and Nick talking together with Tom and Audrey in view but not earshot. Charlie in an exasperated mood; from time to time he steals a half-glance in their direction.

CHARLIE

I don't see how you can stand him. You're always complaining about people being frauds and phoneys. This guy is the phoney of the decade, yet you act as if he were your long-lost best friend.

NICK

Tom's hardly a phoney – just mildly deluded. . . . He's a perfectly nice guy.

CHARLIE

That's just another aspect of his phoniness. He's a terrible phoney, and when he's not being a phoney, he's a bastard.

NICK

Oh, come on.

CHARLIE

You saw how he treated Audrey last night.

NICK

Audrey seems to've forgotten it.

CHARLIE

She has to act that way. Otherwise it would be even more humiliating. But I don't have to pretend Tom Townsend is a nice guy.

NICK

You're really gaga about Audrey, aren't you?

CHARLIE

If by "gaga" you mean, do I like her? Yes, I do.

NICK

Well, why don't you do something about it, instead of just going on and on about what a "bastard" Tom Townsend is.

CHARLIE

What do I do? Declare myself? . . . That would be an absolute disaster. – Don't think I haven't thought about these things. – But I think if the situation could just continue as it has been, then gradually, over time, it'd grow into something more. That, at least, is what I've been hoping for.

INT. FOWLER APARTMENT – NIGHT

Cynthia, Sally, Fred, Tom.

213

CYNTHIA

(*Replying to Sally*) Yes, Rick and Serena broke up, but this afternoon they both went down to Washington for Holly Gilchrist's party. It was Holly who was responsible for them getting together in the first place.

FRED

What a responsibility.

TOM

(*Casually*) They went together?

Nick enters the room holding carefully a too-full cocktail.

CYNTHIA

They "went" separately; how they'll come back . . . I don't think Rick is the sort of guy who lets himself be "dropped."

SALLY

You think Serena dropped him?

CYNTHIA

That's what she wants everyone to think.

At this Nick snorts cynically.

What's that supposed to mean?

Nick repeats sound.

Rick really threatens you somehow.

NICK

How does he threaten me?

CYNTHIA

Maybe by being more of a man than you are.

NICK

(*Taken aback*) . . . you stupid slut . . .

SALLY

Come on –

CYNTHIA

– No, if Nick is going to always be viciously attacking Rick he

should be prepared to take some criticism himself. What's
Rick done that's so terrible?

NICK

He is terrible. I shouldn't have to go into all the sordid details.

FRED

Could you go into a few sordid details?

CYNTHIA

I don't think there are any reasons, except maybe jealousy.
Rick makes him feel terribly inadequate somehow.

NICK

(*Calling her bluff*) Okay, I'll tell you about Von
Sloneker. . . . Does the name Polly Perkins mean anything to
you?

AUDREY

It sounds familiar.

NICK

She grew up in Virgina, a horse fanatic since childhood, and
went away to one of the horsey girls' schools – Garrison
Forest, I think. Sometime in her senior year she started feeling
depressed – partly it was finally becoming disillusioned with
horses, but there were some real psychological problems, too.

That summer she got a job in Edgartown and seemed
completely recovered except for a couple of idiosyncracies:
she'd dress only in blue and wouldn't eat hamburgers unless
they were completely well-done – any hint of redness and she
would send them back. Out of loyalty to her boyfriend in
Virginia she'd only go out on group dates, never individual
ones.

Von Sloneker met her when he came to Edgartown for the
Regatta. She showed no interest in him at all initially, which
makes sense because he's a completely uninteresting guy.
(*Cynthia makes a face at this.*) But for someone like Von
Sloneker that's just inciting, so he swung into action with the
full rigmarole of how desperately in love he was, that she was
the only girl who'd ever made him feel that way, that it was
their obligation to live life to the fullest.

215

Girls are deeply impressed when some total bastard tells them stuff they'd consider comical coming from a normal guy.

SALLY

You can't make generalizations like that.

NICK

Von Sloneker accomplished his objective, which quenched his devotion pretty completely. Polly had meanwhile quit her job and joined his boat for the rest of the cruise, but now he ignored her completely. She of course became obsessed with him and, under the influence of vast quantities of alcohol, willing to submit to the most disgusting abuse.

Do you all know what "pulling a train" means?

AUDREY

I don't think so.

NICK

When Von Sloneker had gotten her blind drunk one night he talked her into pulling a train for him, Victor Lemley and the other crew members.

Shocked murmurs from the Rat Pack.

When Polly arrived at Wheaton for her first semester she was acting very strangely, wearing the same clothes all the time and apparently not washing, just putting on more and more make-up and perfume. She'd remain silent for hours and then talk obsessively about Paul McCartney. After two weeks she was moved to McLean's for treatment, but was able to go home to Virginia for Thanksgiving. The day after Thanksgiving she went into their stables and killed herself.

CYNTHIA

I've heard about that girl and it wasn't Rick's fault. She was just some girl who had a crush on him but whom he hardly knew. She'd always had psychological problems and was, in fact, a pathological liar. It was very sad what happened but Rick had absolutely nothing to do with it.

216

NICK

I don't know. She was carrying his photo when she killed
herself.

CYNTHIA

That doesn't mean anything.

EXT. PARK AVENUE — NIGHT/PRE-DAWN

*Tom and Nick walking uptown from Sally's. Camera follows them for
a few moments while they are not saying anything.*

TOM

What an appalling story.

NICK

Yeah.

TOM

Not many people could know about it – Von Sloneker could
hardly show his face around here. . . . And you really showed
up Cynthia. Whew.

NICK

Yeah, that's what made it worthwhile for me.

TOM

What do you mean?

NICK

There wasn't any Polly Perkins.

TOM

What?

NICK

I made it up. There was no girl.

TOM

You're kidding.

NICK

I couldn't let Cynthia get away with all that nonsense about
Von Sloneker. . . . And basically it's all true. Von Sloneker has

done all those things and worse, though "Polly Perkins" is essentially a composite, based on real people, like *New York Magazine* does.

> TOM
> But Cynthia said she knew all about her.

> NICK
> Yeah, I know. That was priceless. I think it just shows that Von Sloneker is doing those kinds of things all the time.

> TOM
> But you really do have some factual basis for saying all those things about him. It's not just some personal –

> NICK
> Of course there's a factual basis to it.

Fade to black.

DAY SIX

TITLE CARD: Manhattan's Upper East Side – Christmas Eve Day

Montage of daytime Upper East Side street scenes.

EXT. MADISON AVENUE BETWEEN 77TH AND 78TH STREETS – DAY

Facade of bookshop. Audrey appears walking up avenue and enters.

EXT. /INT. BOOKSHOP – DAY

Audrey with shopping bags looking in window, then enters, diffidently approaches the CLERK, *a graduate student type bored with the shop's bourgeois clientele.*

AUDREY

By any chance, would you have any book on the French social philosopher Fourier?

CLERK

I doubt it. You might try in the back.

EXT. IN FRONT OF BENDEL'S — DAY

Jane and Audrey with shopping bags, talking before each goes in separate direction.

JANE

. . . still obsessed with Serena. You're actually much better off not being involved with a guy who's clearly so mixed-up [— he's not going to be good news for anyone for a long time]. . . .

EXT. FIFTH AVENUE — LATE AFTERNOON

Audrey walking past Rockefeller Center Christmas Tree, through hordes of shoppers, looking tragic with very sad music on soundtrack.

EXT. OR INT. BROOKS BROTHERS (OR ANY SIMILAR MEN'S STORE) — LATE AFTERNOON

Forlorn Audrey looking at tie counter. Music continues.

INT. ST. THOMAS EPISCOPAL CHURCH — NIGHT

Start of Christmas Eve Carol Service.

EXT. ST. THOMAS CHURCH STEPS — NIGHT

Audrey, trailing her family into the church, runs into Serena and they talk on the way inside.

SERENA

I was talking with Tom Townsend the other night; he spoke very highly of you.

AUDREY

Really?

SERENA

Yes. (*Pauses – can't quite remember what it was.*) He said you were . . . very . . . well read.

AUDREY

Oh.

INT. ST. THOMAS CHURCH – NIGHT

Procession of boys' choir. Majestic ceremony. Beautiful Christmas music.

INT. ST. THOMAS CHURCH BALCONY – NIGHT

Audrey among her family group singing, tears streaming down her face.

INT. TOWNSEND MAID'S ROOM (TOM'S ROOM) – NIGHT

Close-up of old black-and-white TV screen showing WPIX Channel 11's traditional Christmas Eve broadcast – a yule log burning in a fireplace with Christmas music playing in the background.

Tom, wearing ill-fitting wrapper, goes through box of old school papers, photos and letters. From the morass of papers he throws some saved school newspapers away and retrieves two photos of Serena, which he rests along the wall.

Fade to black.

TITLE CARD: December 25 – Traditional Christmas celebrated.

Fade to black.

TITLE CARD: December 26 – "Orgy Week" begins.

INT. CLARKE LIVING ROOM — NIGHT

Two green-felt-covered bridge tables have been set up with eight chairs around them. Present or soon entering from outside the room are all the SFRPers except Tom (Jane, Sally, Audrey, Cynthia, Nick, Charlie and Fred). Fred shuffling cards, Charlie reading a book, Sally looking at her reflection in something other than a mirror, and Nick looking at the books on the Clarkes' bookshelves. A Fred Astaire record plays on the phonograph. Jane sets a pencil and pad of paper on each table; Audrey takes her place at one of the tables. Nick is examining the titles when he finds one of particular interest and pulls it out.

NICK

(After looking at book jacket, to Jane:) So you're familiar with Dr. Pomeroy's work?

JANE

Who?

NICK

(Reading) "*Girls and Sex* by Wardell B. Pomeroy. . . . The long-needed modern guide to the understanding of girls growing up." Quote: "The most frank and objective book currently available. – Library Journal."

JANE

(A bit embarrassed) Oh, that.

FRED

(Changing subject) You know, we don't have two tables. There're only seven of us.

JANE

That's impossible.

NICK

Tom isn't here yet.

CHARLIE

Is he coming?

NICK

Sure. *(To Jane:)* He's coming, isn't he?

JANE

Uh . . .

AUDREY

(*Upset*) You didn't call him?

JANE

I thought there were eight of us – he'd have been the ninth.

AUDREY

You told me . . .

NICK

Just give him a call. I'm sure he's not doing anything else.

CHARLIE

Surely there's someone in New York who can play bridge other than Tom Townsend. You know, seven can play.

SALLY

What have you against Tom?

CHARLIE

Just one thing: He's not a good person.

NICK

What nonsense.

CHARLIE

I don't care – go ahead and call him if you want.

SALLY

Actually I don't think Tom approves of bridge. But we should ask him anyway.

INT. CLARKE LIVING ROOM – NIGHT

Camera follows Tom arriving. Before him is a tableau of all the SFRPers, sitting patiently at the two card tables, watching as he comes in.

INT. CLARKE LIVING ROOM – NIGHT

Nick, Tom, Audrey and Jane playing at one table.

JANE

(*Instructing Tom*) Just say you pass.

TOM

I pass . . .

NICK

Two clubs.

TOM

I couldn't believe you were actually going to play bridge. It's such a bourgeois cliché.

NICK

That's exactly why I play. I don't enjoy it one bit.

INT. CLARKE LIVING ROOM – NIGHT

Much later, the card tables have disappeared and not so many lights are on. Tom and Audrey in conversation on the sofa.

TOM

I intended to go and got as far as the door.

AUDREY

What happened?

TOM

My mother got upset. She said she couldn't face being alone on Christmas Eve – that it was very important to her that the family be together then. I pointed out to her that two people were hardly a family, but that must have been tactless, because she started crying. My brother never comes home for Christmas anymore.

So, anyway, I stayed and just had a traditional Christmas with Channel Eleven's traditional yule log. For me, and for probably a lot of people, that is Christmas in New York.

AUDREY

Oh, yeah, I think I've seen that.

TOM

My parents' separation agreement stipulates that at noon on

223

Christmas Day we go to my father's place. This year I was actually a bit reluctant to go, because I hadn't been able to get through to him all week, but my mother insisted that the agreement be followed to the letter.

It was a real nightmare. First, the doormen at my father's building wouldn't even let me up – I guess they didn't remember me from Christmas two years ago. Then there was a lot of confusion and whispering until finally it turned out he wasn't there at all and they gave me a piece of paper with a Santa Fé, New Mexico, address on it.

They said he had moved to Santa Fé. I couldn't believe it. . . . They took me up to the apartment. Except for the papers and litter and wire coathangers lying around it was completely empty. He hadn't told me anything about moving. It was quite a surprise.

AUDREY

(*Very sympathetic*) That's awful. There must be some explanation. He must have written you or something and the letter was delayed.

TOM

I don't know.

AUDREY

And your relationship with him was so good.

TOM

In retrospect, I wonder how good it was. I hadn't seen him since last spring. Maybe I was kidding myself.

To avoid mawkishness changes topic, but voice still breaks.

Oh, I've been reading Jane Austen – *Persuasion*. I like it. It's quite . . . (*surprised*) funny.

AUDREY

That's why people like her.

TOM

I was surprised. . . .

DAY NINE

*Sally, Jane and Audrey entering like habitués and going straight to the
photos for the last dances before Christmas.*

> SALLY
>
> (*Looking at photo*) Doesn't Serena look awful here. She's not
> exactly photogenic.

> JANE
>
> (*To Audrey:*) There was one of you and Tom. (*Looks for it.*)
> Here.

*Audrey looks, with emotion, at the photo of her and Tom together at a
dance the week before – happier days.*

INT. TOWNSEND KITCHEN — DAY

*In contrast to his daytime college slob look of the week before, Tom is
now wearing a tie, something approaching a suit, and has his hair
combed back wet, as if he were a preppie who had recently showered.
He is finishing a cup of coffee while reading the paper. Mrs. Townsend
stands nearby.*

> MRS. TOWNSEND
>
> I don't think you should feel that your father's moving without
> telling you means that he doesn't care about you.

INT. CLARKE APARTMENT — NIGHT

*Nick and others in semi-casual clothes; Fred, the only one with a job,
wears a suit.*

> NICK
>
> The titled aristocracy are the scum of the earth. What really
> makes me furious is the idea of a whole class of people, mostly
> Europeans, all looking down on me.

> FRED
>
> What about the Duke of Earl?

SALLY

You always say "titled" aristocrats. Are there *untitled* aristocrats?

Nick takes a deep bow.

CYNTHIA

You're *so* conceited.

CHARLIE

Saying that the titled aristocracy is the scum of the earth is, obviously, an exaggeration – but it's true that the forces that oblige members of the UHB to at least appear to act productively and responsibly carry little weight, or none at all, with people whose social position is publicly acknowledged and secure no matter what they do – the titled aristocracy.

INT. CLARKE APARTMENT – NIGHT

Later. Rat Pack sitting around partially clothed, playing strip poker and discussing Tom's disinheritance. Audrey and Charlie are out of the game, and perhaps playing chess to the side.

NICK

So you had a trust fund. The pieces are beginning to fall into place.

TOM

Well, I don't have one anymore.

CHARLIE

That's less important sociologically. What's important is having grown up with the assumption of material security. It explains a lot.

SALLY

(*Concentrating on her cards*) I call.

They all show their cards. Sally has nothing. Jane is high. The others all take off a layer of clothing.

NICK

(*To Sally:*) You had no cards – why did you call?

226

SALLY

I felt like it.

NICK

Playing strip poker with an exhibitionist somehow takes the challenge away.

INT. CLARKE APARTMENT – NIGHT

Somewhat later Tom, now fully dressed, and Audrey talk. Other Rat Packers are nearby.

TOM

I tried not to think about it – the assumption being that it wouldn't really amount to much anyway. Yet I think it did affect how I looked at everything.

AUDREY

(*Sympathetic*) Yes, I think it does.

TOM

Actually, it's a tremendous relief – not having that hanging over me anymore. There was a big load of guilt that went with it, even though it wasn't that much money and I never really counted on having it.

NICK

(*From farther off, interjecting comments*) You're a tragic case. You've just been robbed and it's a great relief to you.

TOM

(*Grave*) In a way it is. (*Continues, in conversation with Audrey.*) At least, regarding the money; regarding my relationship with my father I'm of course concerned. He moves to another state without telling me, doesn't call or write for months and basically has me disinherited. Obviously our relationship was not what I thought it was.

NICK

(*Again, from afar: a cackle or exclamation – "sheez."*)

227

TOM

No contact at all. Not a word. It's as if he were incredibly angry with me but I can't think of why. I don't know what it could be.

NICK

You don't?

TOM

No . . . well . . . no.

NICK

One word – "stepmother."

TOM

Well, I hope I can talk to them and straighten things out.

NICK

I'm sure nothing you said or did had anything to do with this, and nothing you say or do now will change anything.

SALLY

That's awfully pessimistic.

NICK

That's just the way things are. The most important thing to realize about parents is that there's absolutely nothing you can do about them.

Everyone turns toward the staircase. Coming down from the floor above is Fred, apparently quite drunk, and still largely undressed from the strip-poker game. The most striking aspect of his appearance is his wearing, around his chest, a large brassiere. Descending the stairs with great dignity and walking carefully across the Clarke living room, he finally flops on the sofa, leaning back, almost passed out.

It's quite becoming.

FRED
(*Looking down at his chest*) You like it?

SALLY

This is really decadent.

This is nothing.

Fred has evidently passed out. They look at him.

TOM

Maybe it's what you said before – just Fred's way of coping
with all the happiness at home.

Fade to black.

DAY TEN

INT. TOWNSEND APARTMENT – DAY

Tom talking on the kitchen phone, conversation in progress.

TOM

. . . [I went there] on Christmas Day and learned you'd moved
from the doorman. . . . How could you go without telling me –
I was in town. . . . What's happened? . . . That's not
true. . . . Will you let me talk to her. . . . If she says that, she's
crazy. . . . (*chastened*) I do take it back, I'm sorry; it's just
that . . . No, I don't. . . . How can you treat me this
way? . . . Dad? . . . Dad? . . . Dad? . . .

*Tom, hung up upon, returns the phone to its receiver. He paces, tense
and preoccupied, around the kitchen.*

INT. CLARKE FOYER

*Tom waiting on elevator landing in front of the door to Clarke
apartment; Audrey opens the door and motions to Tom to hurry
inside.*

AUDREY

(*Dramatically*) Something's happened to Nick.

*They walk to Clarke library where Nick is seated on sofa. Some other
SFRPers are around. Nick grasps his head tightly with both hands.*

NICK

(*In a strange, tense, almost ridiculously weird voice*) It's my head!

JANE

What?

NICK

It's my head! My head!

The other SFRPers look on, perplexed.

TOM

What's going on?

CHARLIE

There was a guy at school Nick liked to imitate saying this. He had taken mescaline and then went around doing this about his head.

TOM

Nick took mescaline?

CHARLIE

No, this other guy – Voss.

NICK

The mesc . . . My head!

It's hard to tell whether Nick's partly joking or entirely serious. But his tone is disturbingly intense, and the other SFRPers look worried.

CYNTHIA

We did take some mescaline.

JANE

You what?

CYNTHIA

He shouldn't be reacting this way, though. I don't know what's happened to him. It was very mild.

NICK

My head! It's my head!

CHARLIE

Are you joking?

Nick shakes his head "no" and looks grim.

INT. CLARKE LIVING ROOM — NIGHT

Quite a while later. Sally has placed an empty highball glass on the coffee table, other SFRPers sit around her. Nick sits, subdued but apparently recovered from his mescaline experience, looking intently at the illustrations in an oversized book.

> SALLY
>
> It's called "Truth." You stretch a Kleenex over the mouth of a highball glass and place a dime on it, then we take turns burning a hole in it with a cigarette; if the dime falls in on your turn you lose and have to answer with absolute honesty whatever question you're asked, no matter how embarrassing.

> CYNTHIA
>
> Yes, the more embarrassing the better.

INT. CORNER OF CLARKE LIVING ROOM — NIGHT

> JANE
>
> What are you reading?

> NICK
>
> (*His manner greatly changed, his voice tremulous and sweet*) The Story of Babar . . . (*his eyes tearing*) . . . I forgot how beautiful it was (*choked with emotion*).

INT. CLARKE LIVING ROOM — NIGHT

Broad scene as previously, Sally and co. preparing for "Truth."

> CYNTHIA
>
> (*Excited*) [Sometimes you find out the] most amazing things. It can be really incredible.

> AUDREY
>
> I don't think we should play this.

> SALLY
>
> Why not?

231

AUDREY

There are good reasons why people don't go around telling each other their most intimate thoughts.

CYNTHIA

What do you have to hide?

AUDREY

No, I just know that games like this can be really dangerous.

TOM

(*Skeptical*) "Dangerous"?

SALLY

I don't see what's "dangerous" about it.

AUDREY

You don't have to. Other people have. That's how it became a convention – people saw the harm excessive candor could do. That's why there are conventions, so people don't have to go around repeating the same mistakes over and over again.

CYNTHIA

You admit that it's basically just a social convention, then.

SALLY

(*To Audrey:*) What you say might be true among people who don't know each other well, but surely not with us.

AUDREY

Then it's even worse.

CYNTHIA

Let's discuss this. Basically, what this game requires is complete candor – which means openness, honesty. I don't see how that can be bad.

AUDREY

Well, it can.

CYNTHIA

Then don't play – but don't wreck it for everyone else.

SALLY

No, if we're going to play, we all should, that's the whole point.

CHARLIE

If one of us doesn't want to play, I don't think any of us should. . . . Maybe Audrey's right.

NICK

(*In his new passive, sweet post-Babar tone*) Oh, come on, let's not disagree. You're really both saying the same thing: either we all play, or none of us should.

CYNTHIA

It's really all up to Audrey, then.

There's a long pause during which nearly everyone looks at Audrey for some response; she looks down, pondering the situation.

CHARLIE

This isn't fair –

AUDREY

No. Go ahead. I'll play.

MONTAGE

Cigarette burning holes in tissue. Moving clockwise from Sally, who goes first, all through Fred take turns without incident. Then on Cynthia's try, she moves the cigarette clumsily and the coin drops. She seems a bit exhilarated, perhaps somewhat pleased to be the first victim.

FRED

What now?

CYNTHIA

You ask me any question you want.

FRED

And what's second prize? . . . Okay, I'm supposed to ask you the most embarrassing question I can think of. . . . Uhhh . . . what's the most embarrassing thing that's ever happened to you?

233

                              SALLY
   No, something specific. . . .

Fred gives her a blank look. He is embarrassed.

   "Who was your most recent conquest"? Something like that.

                              FRED
   Who was your most recent conquest?

                            CYNTHIA
   You mean whom did I sleep with last?

                            CHARLIE
   You don't have to answer that.

                            CYNTHIA
   It doesn't embarrass me. I've nothing to hide. . . . It was Nick.

*Nick is embarrassed, though still dazed. All look at him in surprise.
Jane is the most obviously affected.*

                              JANE
   After all that about what a terrible slut she was.

                              NICK
   But a very attractive slut.

                            CHARLIE
   So you're just another hypocrite.

                              NICK
   That's not hypocrisy. It's sin.

                            CYNTHIA
   It was hardly that.

Jane is silent but angry.

MONTAGE

*Showing again cigarettes burning holes in a new tissue. This time the
coin drops on Tom's turn. He looks appalled.*

                              234

JANE

I've got a question. . . . (*A pause for phrasing.*) With absolute honesty and frankness, list all the girls you are interested in romantically, in descending order of interest, and why, including significant detail.

TOM

I thought that was pretty obvious. I've had a crush on Serena, with some ups and downs, for over two years. Recently it seems to have developed into something more serious.

Audrey's face remains exaggeratedly expressionless.

CYNTHIA

But who else do you like, romantically?

TOM

(*Pauses*) I don't think it works that way. If you're really interested in one person, you're not interested in anyone else. Well, maybe it's possible, but what's the point?

Audrey is silent and expressionless; she looks down at a bracelet and fiddles with it.

CYNTHIA

And if it doesn't work out? There must be someone else.

TOM

If it doesn't work out this time, I'll be off romance for a long time.

FRED

I suppose this is embarrassing, but it's hardly a revelation.

Audrey abruptly and hurriedly leaves the room, her head down.

INT. JANE'S ROOM — NIGHT

Jane and Audrey, who has been crying.

JANE

I'm sorry I asked him that. It was my fault.

235

AUDREY

I always think other people are foolish. I'm the big fool.

INT. CLARKE KITCHEN — NIGHT

Jane and Cynthia.

CYNTHIA

It's better for her to know the truth. I don't see how knowing the truth can do anyone any "harm."

JANE

The truth she would've found out anyway. But she would've learned it without the maximum of embarrassment and pain. It's not just the truth — it's how and when you learn it.

CYNTHIA

I don't accept that.

INT. CLARKE APARTMENT — NIGHT

Charlie finds Audrey alone and approaches her.

CHARLIE

You were right about that "game" — it's terrible. . . . You might not realize it, Audrey, but everyone admires you a lot.

AUDREY

Thank you, but I find that very hard to believe.

CHARLIE

It's true — and it's not just because you're smart and good-looking and charming and have principles. No, it's because they can see that you're a good person.

AUDREY

If you want to tease me, this is not the best time.

CHARLIE

I'm completely sincere. . . . (*Pause.*) Maybe this isn't the best time to tell you, but for some time now I . . . I like you very much. I know you don't yet feel —

AUDREY

(*Interrupting*) No – please stop!

Very upset, involuntarily covers her face and bolts from the room – for Audrey the evening has been a complete nightmare.

Fade to black.

DAY ELEVEN

INT. ROUGET APARTMENT – DAY

Jane paints her toenails while Audrey talks. Or both painting their toenails.

AUDREY

Maybe Cynthia's right.

JANE

That's impossible.

AUDREY

Her essential view is that experience is good, and she's set out to acquire it. I've been just the opposite. Everything's been in my imagination – all the romance imaginary, nothing real.

JANE

She's a slut.

AUDREY

That's what Nick says.

JANE

He proved it.

AUDREY

That's unfair.

JANE

I don't think so.

237

INT. CLARKE APARTMENT – NIGHT

Tom talking with Nick, who's dressed in white tie and has with him a small old-fashioned suitcase.

> NICK
>
> I'm getting the dawn train upstate – to East Aurora, my father's place. It's the first time they've invited me in years – and I can't help wondering why my stepmother's suddenly willing to have me come. . . . If I should die while there, would you see that there's a thorough investigation – even if it looks like an accident or natural causes?

Tom chuckles at this, assuming Nick is wholly in jest.

> Would you promise that?

> TOM
>
> Yes.

> NICK
>
> Even if I return alive, I don't think I'll be attending any more dances after this one. With everything that's going on, this is probably the last deb season as we know it. I don't want to just hang around watching the decline.

> TOM
>
> (*Worried*) Everyone's going tonight?

> NICK
>
> (*Emphatically*) No. . . . (*Explaining.*) Just me. The International is an inorganic debutante ball. The others were natural outgrowths of local UHB formations. This was assembled like a tourist attraction. Each girl has two escorts, one a cadet in uniform from one of the service academies, the other a civilian, like me. The pretension is that each deb represents some state or country. A military fellow carrying its flag precedes her at the presentation. And the whole thing is televised on Channel Nine.

> TOM
>
> You're kidding.

NICK

No. It's vulgar – I like it a lot. And these Texas and Oklahoma debs are really nice – a real relief from these hypercritical New York girls.

TOM

What's everyone else doing, then?

NICK

I imagine they'll be glued to the set (*indicates Clarke TV set*).

INT. CLARKE APARTMENT – NIGHT

Some time later. From a distance traveling camera approaches a somewhat reduced group of SFRPers – Sally, Jane, Charlie and Tom awake; Fred asleep – in Clarke library loosely gathered around the TV set, from which a master of ceremonies' voice can be heard.

ANNOUNCER (*o.s., TV*)

From the state of Tennessee, Miss Sabina Johnston, daughter of Mr. and Mrs. Roderick Johnston of Memphis and Southampton.

The orchestra plays Tennessee state anthem.

SALLY

She's cute.

JANE

But what about the dress.

They continue watching the television.

TOM

Nick said he thought this would be the last real deb season.

SALLY

How come?

TOM

Because of everything going on.

SALLY

What?

TOM

Well – everything.

CHARLIE

The stock market, the economy, contemporary social attitudes . . . But over the long run they could be doomed for another reason. The parties take a lot of work and organization. This has traditionally been done by elderly ladies commonly referred to as the "Old Biddies." But the Old Biddies aren't getting any younger. When they start to disappear, who's going to take their place? I don't think there's anyone.

TOM

That's interesting – it's the sort of thing no one ever thinks of. . . .
    Is Audrey coming tonight?

JANE

She was really tired and thought she'd stay home – she can watch Channel Nine equally well from there.

Buzz from house telephone.

Uhps, maybe that's her now.

She goes to the phone.

ANNOUNCER (*o.s., TV*)

From the State of Oklahoma, Miss Carol Ann Dawson, daughter of Mr. and Mrs. Wallace Beveridge of Tulsa, and Mr. Thomas Dawson of Fort Lauderdale, Florida.

The orchestra plays the Oklahoma state anthem.

Jane returns.

JANE

Cynthia's coming up with Rick Von Sloneker. . . . She'd mentioned they might come by.

TOM

What would Nick say?

JANE

What Nick says or thinks, I couldn't care less.

INT. CLARKE APARTMENT — NIGHT

Shortly later. Cynthia has arrived with Rick Von Sloneker and VICTOR
LEMLEY, *and is introducing them to Tom, the only one there they*
wouldn't know.

CYNTHIA

. . . Rick Von Sloneker and Victor Lemley . . .

All shake hands.

TOM

(*To Von Sloneker:*) I've heard a lot about you.

VON SLONEKER

Of course you have. . . . Who was talking about me? . . . Nick
Smith?

Tom nods "yes."

That jerk. I don't see how anyone can take him seriously.

VICTOR LEMLEY

He's just a jerk.

The phone rings and Jane goes to get it.

CYNTHIA

I think he feels incredibly threatened by you or something.

VON SLONEKER

What a clown.

TOM

Is it true you're a baron?

VON SLONEKER

As a matter of fact, it is. I don't take that sort of thing
seriously, though.

JANE

(*Returning*) That was Audrey – she is coming.

VON SLONEKER

Audrey Rouget? She's getting pretty attractive.

VICTOR LEMLEY

(*About telecast*) What's this?

SALLY

The International.

CHARLIE

(*Sententiously, looking at watch*) In a little more than an hour the season will be over.

VON SLONEKER

You really take that sort of thing seriously. I can't.

TOM

There are a lot of things you don't take very seriously. One could get the impression you're not a very serious person.

VON SLONEKER

(*With a look of disbelief*) Who is this guy? Some Nick Smith impersonator? . . . I was sick of it from the original.

CYNTHIA

Yeah, Tom, cut it out. That's gotten really tiresome. The things Nick said were completely untrue.

INT. CLARKE APARTMENT — NIGHT

Audrey and Charlie in isolated part of apartment.

AUDREY

I'm sorry about last night. I didn't mean what I said.

CHARLIE

(*Very pleased*) No, it was idiotic of me to approach you that way. I hadn't intended to.

AUDREY

It wasn't idiotic.

INT. FOYER OUTSIDE APARTMENT — NIGHT

The elevator door opens. A girl in a long white dress, SABINA
JOHNSTON, *and a West Point cadet,* GEORGE FRAWLEY, *leave the
elevator, followed by Nick, who presses the Clarkes' doorbell.*

INT. CLARKE APARTMENT — NIGHT

Nick introduces his guests to the others.

> NICK
>
> . . . Miss Sabina Johnston of Memphis and Cadet Lieutenant
> George Frawley of – West Point.

INT. CLARKE APARTMENT — NIGHT

*Wide view of the whole room with all the guests, Nick at one end and
Von Sloneker at the other.*

> NICK
>
> (*In a loud voice to Jane:*) I go away for a few hours and you get
> Von Sloneker up here.

> JANE
>
> I can invite anyone I want.

> NICK
>
> Oh, so you invited him.

> JANE
>
> I didn't, but even if I had, it's none of your business.

> NICK
>
> How can you say that – you know what kind of guy he is.

> JANE
>
> I don't – it's only what you say, and you're completely
> untrustworthy.

> NICK
>
> Not about something serious.

> VON SLONEKER
>
> (*In a loud voice from across the room*) Smith, you're a liar.

243

The room becomes silent

I've heard all the crap you've been telling about me.

NICK

(*As if flattered*) You have?

VON SLONEKER

About some girl I supposedly mistreated – Polly Perkins.
There is no Polly Perkins. You know that.

A prolonged silence.

Tell them. You made it up.

Nick remains silent.

JANE

Is that true?

NICK

Yes and no.

CHARLIE

Oh, God, Nick.

JANE

You did make it up.

NICK

There is no one Polly Perkins. . . . There're many of them.

VON SLONEKER

(*Very aggressive*) So you admit you lied.

NICK

"Polly Perkins" is a composite – like *New York Magazine*
does –

VON SLONEKER

– Name one.

NICK

Girls who've already been degraded by you don't need the
further humiliation of having their names bandied about non-
exclusive Park Avenue afterparties.

VON SLONEKER

You see? There's no one.

CHARLIE

That looks really bad, Nick.

Silence – Nick on the ropes, the crowd has turned against him.

NICK

– Cathy Livingstone. No more harm can be done to her.
She's beyond the reach of the gossips now.

VON SLONEKER

I had nothing to do with that. She was completely unstable.

NICK

That didn't stop you from boozing her up and talking her into
pulling a train for you and Lemley.

VON SLONEKER

That's not what happened!

NICK

What happened, Ricky?

VON SLONEKER

Anything which went on between Cathy Livingstone and me
was entirely personal, entirely private, and has nothing to do
with her suicide, which was months afterwards.

NICK

She kept calling and trying to see you, but you wouldn't even
talk to her.

VON SLONEKER

I liked Cathy, but sometimes things don't work out. A clean
break is usually the best.

NICK

Spare us the fake sensitivity. Are her panties still in your
collection? Rick keeps a collection of the panties of the girls
he's seduced. When they later kill themselves, do you do
anything special to memorialize them?

VON SLONEKER

I don't let anyone say that kind of thing to my face.

NICK

Before you complained that I said it behind your back, now it's that it's to your face. . . . Frankly, how can you tell which is which?

Von Sloneker hits Nick in the face. Blood starts pouring out of his nose. Everyone is very surprised, especially Nick.

VON SLONEKER

He's had that coming for a long time.

INT. CLARKE APARTMENT — NIGHT

The group is much reduced: Cynthia, Von Sloneker and Lemley have left. Nick slumps on the sofa holding a bloody handkerchief to his nose and trying to keep his nose high.

NICK

How dare he hit me. He's the scoundrel. *I* should've thrashed *him*.

FRED

Well, you missed your chance.

NICK

I would have if I hadn't been doing my damnedest not to splatter blood all over your apartment. When I got back he was gone. No one does anything to help. I'm facing one of the worst guys of modern times and all I get is whining criticism, (*mimics*) "This looks really bad, Nick."

JANE

Why should we believe you over Rick? We know you're a hypocrite. We know your "Polly Perkins" story was a fabrication –

NICK

– a composite –

246

JANE

— that you're completely impossible and out-of-control with some sort of drug problem and a fixation on what you consider Rick Von Sloneker's wickedness. You're a snob, a sexist, totally obnoxious and tiresome. And lately you've gotten just weird. Why should we believe anything you say?

NICK

I'm not "tiresome."

JANE

(*Disagreeing*) Hunh!

SALLY

(*To Nick, querulously:*) What's Rick to you?

NICK

Your shy friend hits me in the face; I'm about to go upstate to the domain of a stepmother of untrammeled malevolence – very possibly to be killed – and I get this.

JANE

Who could blame her. . . . (*Looking around.*) If not splattering blood was your objective, you weren't terribly successful.

NICK

(*Stands*) Well, I'm going to Grand Central. The people are friendlier.

TOM

(*Stands*) I'll help you with your stuff.

Cadet Lt. Frawley stands to help also. Tom indicates the others.

Why don't we all go see Nick off?

Sabina Johnston, enthusiastic, gets up to join Tom, but no one else does. They are all to some degree fed up with Nick; Fred has again dozed off.

EXT. CURB ADJACENT TO CLARKE BUILDING — DAWN

Nick talking with Tom while waiting for cab.

NICK

Even within this group, there are certain standards. Apparently I failed to live up to them.

INT. GRAND CENTRAL PLATFORMS — EARLY MORNING

Nick still in his tails, Sabina in her evening dress, Cadet Frawley in his dress uniform; only Tom is in civilian clothes.

NICK

(*To Sabina:*) Thank you for coming.

Gives her a kiss on the cheek.

Will you write?

SABINA

Yes.

NICK

(*To Cadet Frawley:*) Goodbye. Thanks for coming.

CADET FRAWLEY

Goodbye, sir.

NICK

Bye, Tom.

TOM

Good luck.

NICK

(*Taking Tom somewhat aside*) I leave counting on you and Charlie to maintain the standards and ideals of the UHB. I've obviously failed to. You and Charlie are the only ones who understand this kind of thing.

TOM

What?

NICK

Also, you remember, in case I die –

TOM

– Yes.

248

Nick, satisfied, starts walking backward toward train, with his suitcase in one hand, with the other waving "farewell" to his friends. He then turns and continues down the platform before turning again and waving back in poignant FDR style.

Fade to black.

DAY TWELVE

MONTAGE

Drum roll on soundtrack. Tom's room. Insert: Calendar with notation, "Serena 7:30." Tom splashing water on his face and looking at himself in the mirror. Repeats, "Tom. Tommy. Tom. Tommy." *Drum roll continues through following scenes.*

INT. TOWNSEND APARTMENT – DAY

Tom studying the restaurant listings in Cue *magazine. His mother passes by.*

                              TOM
Is the "21" Club very expensive?

                         MRS. TOWNSEND
I believe so.

INT. MAID'S BATHROOM – EVENING

Tom finishes shaving, rinses remaining foam from his face and examines what remains of his beard with a disappointed look. He starts relathering his face to shave a second time.

EXT. "21" – NIGHT

The door opens and Serena and Tom come out. Both are in very high spirits – Tom is laughing.

249

                    TOM

That's priceless.

                  SERENA

And then she told Miss Rathbun, "They look awfully big for
mice!"

Tom and Serena laugh more as they reach the sidewalk and head east.

                    TOM

And she believed it?

                  SERENA

Oh, completely.

                    TOM

That's priceless.

They continue down the street in high spirits.

INT. FREY'S BAR — NIGHT

Tom and Serena in a serious conversation.

                  SERENA

You really seem to love Princeton.

                    TOM

Yes. It's great – really beautiful. (*Long pause, then in a very
serious tone.*) Actually, I've felt really depressed since getting
there.

                  SERENA

Really?

                    TOM

Initially I was ecstatic – the refrain "these are the best years of
your life" kept running through my mind. Then it occurred to
me how depressing that is – if these are the "best" years, then
it's all downhill from here. But it wasn't even that logical. It
was as if a dark cloud had suddenly descended on everything
and all that had seemed positive before now seemed utterly
grim and depressing. Before coming home for Christmas I was

                    250

at rock bottom. Some days I wouldn't even have left my room if I hadn't gotten hungry.

SERENA

How awful.

TOM

Well, it's not really that bad. . . . One thing that worries me, though, is the possibility that this is just what adult life is like – that from now on this is how things will be – which is of course even more depressing. . . . I guess everyone goes through periods like this.

SERENA

No, I don't think so. It sounds pretty unusual to me. . . .

TOM

I shouldn't have mentioned it. It's embarrassing.

SERENA

It's not embarrassing. It's depressing.

A pause during which they watch an ultra-preppie couple pass by and sit at a nearby table.

TOM

You went through some sort of depression your junior year in school, didn't you?

Serena tries to remember but can't.

SERENA

I can't remember anything in particular.

TOM

You mentioned something about it in one of your letters – while I was going through some things over Christmas I found a packet of your old letters.

SERENA

(*Surprised*) You saved my letters?

TOM

Of course. I save all the personal letters I get. Don't you?

SERENA

No.

TOM

You mean you threw out the letters I wrote you?

SERENA

I throw away nearly everything. I don't want to go through life
with all the mail I got when I was sixteen.

TOM

. . . I'm really surprised. If someone goes to the trouble of
writing a real letter, I save it. People don't write many personal
letters anymore.

SERENA

People in boarding school do.

TOM

What if someone who wrote you becomes famous? Those
letters could be the only record of what they were thinking at
that time – crucial for their biographers.

SERENA

Do you expect to have biographies written about you? Anyone
who writes me who expects to become famous should keep
carbons.

TOM

It just seems to me that it's a kind of trust, that if someone
takes the trouble to write you a substantial letter, you not
throw it out.

SERENA

I didn't keep your letters, but I didn't throw them out.

TOM

I don't understand. Is that a riddle?

SERENA

There was a girl at school who had some kind of crush on you.
She came into my room when I was throwing things out, so I
gave her your letters.

                        TOM
Really?

                       SERENA
I know it sounds queer.

                        TOM
And she kept them?

                       SERENA
I'm sure.

                        TOM
How strange. She must be really odd.

                       SERENA
No, she's very nice. In fact, you know her – Audrey Rouget.

Fade to black.

DAY THIRTEEN

INT. JANE'S BEDROOM – NIGHT

Tom talking with Jane while she puts on makeup, maintaining a tone of controlled excitement.

                        TOM
While Serena and I were talking, it was as if, suddenly, clouds
lifted and I could see the last two and a half years stretched out
before me like a panoramic view of a broad valley, seen from a
hillside. That Serena was not interested in me, and probably
never had been, was suddenly perfectly clear, just another fact
which could be accepted unemotionally, with no resentment or
recriminations whatsoever. That the romantic vision I had had
was not based on anything real did not negate that vision. It
was just another aspect of the panorama.

                        JANE
You mean you think you've gotten over Serena again.

                         253

TOM

Yes, but it's different this time. Then I was still intensely involved with her, though in a negative way – full of bitterness. I don't feel that way now.

During his speech, an archaic buzzer sounds – the house intercom connecting the lobby to an antique apparatus hidden away in the kitchen.

JANE

Charlie must be on his way up.

TOM

Damn. There was something I wanted to ask you. . . .

JANE

Yes, what was the "surprising thing" Serena told you?

TOM

You probably already know about it, but I was surprised – about Audrey saving my letters.

JANE

What letters?

TOM

The ones I wrote Serena.

JANE

Audrey saved them? God, how queer.

TOM

Well – it's not so queer, really. Serena was about to throw them out – Audrey apparently didn't think people's letters should be destroyed that way; also, from what Serena said, I think Audrey might have had some sort of vague crush on me going back quite a while.

JANE

Uh-huh . . .

TOM

I knew there was something – but I thought it was just the past week, a function of these parties and, you know, the escort shortage. But the odd thing is that while I was with Serena, who's so good-looking and is really nice –

JANE

Serena's basically a good person.

TOM

– on the big night I'd looked forward to for a week, I started feeling this incredible loneliness being with Serena and nostalgia for all those conversations with Audrey before the big blow-up, and this was before I knew anything about the letters.

He pauses to get Jane's reaction; she looks pensive but says nothing.

There's something really great about being with Audrey – I mean I think I prefer arguing with Audrey to agreeing with Serena or someone else. In fact, I had only had that calmly unemotional perspective on my relationship with Serena for a little while when I started feeling this warm glow at the prospect of seeing Audrey here again tonight.

JANE

Uh-oh . . .

TOM

It really surprised me because I thought that if things didn't work out with Serena this time I'd put that sort of thing on hold for a long time. People shouldn't get married 'til their late twenties and that's a long way off.

JANE

Well, your timing's *really* terrible.

TOM

What do you mean?

The apartment doorbell sounds while Jane is still deep in make-up application.

Damn. I'll get it. (*Turns back at doorway.*) I want to continue this.

INT. CLARKE APARTMENT FOYER — NIGHT

Charlie and Fred arriving.

> CHARLIE
>
> Where's Jane?

> TOM
>
> She's still in her room. What would you like to drink?

> CHARLIE
>
> So you're our host.

> FRED
>
> What do people who don't drink have? Ginger ale, ice water . . . ? I don't know. Maybe a Coke – with an aspirin.

INT. JANE'S ROOM — NIGHT

Charlie, Fred, Tom recently arrived with cocktail glasses.

> FRED
>
> You don't need to put on green eye-shadow for us.

> JANE
>
> It's not for you. I've got a date.

> FRED
>
> A "date"? What's that? It sounds like something from the nineteen fifties.

> CHARLIE
>
> Who's the fellow?

> JANE
>
> None of you know him, and I'd like to keep it that way.

INT. CLARKE KITCHEN — NIGHT

Jane, fully dressed to go out, straightening up; Tom is with her.

> TOM
>
> What did you mean when you said that about my timing being off?

256

JANE

Audrey's gone to Cynthia's in Connecticut for the weekend
and then goes back to France Wednesday. And, besides that,
she thinks you're a total jerk. She hates you.

TOM

She *hates* me?

JANE

Well, she despises you. It's a bit my fault.

INT. CLARKE PANTRY — NIGHT

Fred, Jane, etc.

FRED

(*At house phone*) A "Mr. Andrews" is downstairs for you.

JANE

Say I'll be right down.

CHARLIE

We'll go down with you.

JANE

No you won't.

CHARLIE

We can all go out together.

JANE

No. This is a date. . . .

Jane walks out to the elevator landing and they follow her.

FRED

It seems rude not to go down and check him out.

JANE

Please don't. Feel free to stay here, though – there's plenty of
food and stuff.

TOM

I get the impression you don't want us to come along.

CHARLIE

But it's okay if we stay here and wait for everyone else?

JANE

Sure, but what "everyone else"?

CHARLIE

The rest of the SFRP.

The elevator arrives and Jane gets in.

JANE

You are the SFRP tonight – (*Before the elevator doors close.*)
Oh – could you be out by midnight? Feel free to stay until
then.

The Rat Pack remnant seems stunned to be so abruptly abandoned.

CHARLIE

"Be out by midnight" – what's going on? – Jane's bringing this
guy she hardly knows back for some kind of assignation.

TOM

We don't know that.

FRED

Well . . .

CHARLIE

I'm really surprised at Jane. Some guy asks her out and she
abandons everything. The rest of us can go to heck.

FRED

Where's everyone else? Nick really left Manhattan?

CHARLIE

Sally had something tonight, but I think she was coming back
early.

TOM

The whole Rat Pack thing seems to have disintegrated.

FRED

The Rat Pack is down to the rats.

CHARLIE

This is really depressing. Let's get out of here.

INT. MELON'S-LIKE BAR – NIGHT

Charlie, Tom and Fred at round table with red-checked cloth.

CHARLIE

I guess it's understandable that she'd prefer going out on a date, which offers some romantic promise, even if very slight, than stay with us. Still, it's a bit disappointing. I thought we were better friends than that.

FRED

I wonder whether we're really friends for them, or just way-stations between dates. For them men are all either dates, potential-dates, or date-substitutes. I find that dehumanizing.

CHARLIE

That might be the case with Cynthia or Sally, but Audrey, for instance, is completely different. She's someone who'd keep up her friendships no matter what. Audrey has a rare largeness of mind – she's not obsessed with her love life. Good-looking, smart, charming, principled – it's an unusual combination.

TOM

Yeah, Audrey's great.

CHARLIE

(*Incredulous*) You've got a very peculiar way of showing it.

TOM

What do you mean?

CHARLIE

You've given her nothing but grief all the past week.

TOM

That's not true at all.

FRED

(*Wearily*) Oh, stop it – over and over, the same thing . . .

INT. MELON'S-LIKE BAR — NIGHT

Same scene seconds later.

                    FRED
   I think I'll be going anyway. I have nothing to say. I'm
   completely boring without a drink.

                    TOM
   (*Looks at watch*) It's only midnight – you can't go.

                    FRED
   (*Getting up*) I'm sorry. Without cocktails, staying up all night
   loses its charm. I haven't had anything amusing to say since I
   stopped drinking.

                    TOM
   Did you have anything amusing to say before you stopped?

                    FRED
   I know. But it seemed amusing; now it doesn't.

                    CHARLIE
   You were asleep.

                    FRED
   Was that it?

INT. SAME BAR — NIGHT

*Fred has gone. Tom and Charlie stand with cocktails in hand listening
to the discourse of an aging preppie,* DICK EDWARDS, *sleek but worn-
out-looking for his late forties.*

                    DICK EDWARDS
   When I was in college we would be going to dances over
   Christmas vacation. Do they still go on?

                    CHARLIE
   Yes.

                    EDWARDS
   Probably much reduced, though.

General nodding in agreement.

I wouldn't put much stock in them. You meet a group of people, you like them, you think "these are going to be my friends the rest of my life," then you never see them again. I don't know where they go.

TOM

Do you think it's true that, generally speaking, people from this sort of background are doomed to failure?

EDWARDS

"Doomed"? That would make it easier. We just fail, without being doomed, which is worse.

CHARLIE

You feel you've failed?

EDWARDS

Yeah.

TOM

But you still can afford to come here.

EDWARDS

I'm not destitute. I have a job that pays decently. But it's all mediocre and unimpressive.

The acid test – the acid test – is if you get any pleasure from answering the question, "What do you do?" I can't bear it.

You start out expecting something much more and some of your contemporaries achieve it – you start reading about them in the papers or seeing them on TV. That's one of the dangers of midtown Manhattan, always running into far more successful contemporaries. I try to avoid them if I can. If I can't – they're of course always very friendly. But either they ask what I'm doing, or they think it.

CHARLIE

I find it hard to believe that many people from our background are successful. Aren't you confusing them with people you might have known from college who came from normal backgrounds? It's not surprising that energetic self-confident achievers free of "uhb" illusions should be successful.

EDWARDS

What's "uhb"?

CHARLIE

"Uhb" – UHB – acronym for "urban haute bourgeoisie." It's a more sociologically precise alternative to "preppie" and other terms.

Edwards thinks.

EDWARDS

You're partly right: Some of the successful contemporaries I mentioned were not from an "uhb" background. But some were. You'll have to accept it – not everyone from our background is doomed to failure.

CHARLIE

I wonder whether they were typical "uhbs." There was probably some factor which set them apart. Also, their careers are not over – the failure could still be to come.

EXT. STREET OUTSIDE BAR – NIGHT

Tom and Charlie leaving in overcoats.

TOM

He seems less pessimistic than you.

CHARLIE

I know. It doesn't ring true.

EXT. AVENUE ACROSS FROM SALLY FOWLER'S BUILDING – NIGHT

Tom and Charlie look up at her apartment windows to see that the lights are on. Tom starts walking toward the building.

CHARLIE

You can't just go up to her place unannounced after midnight.

TOM

It all depends who's on the elevator.

CHARLIE

It's not a question of who's on the elevator. You've known
Sally for – what? – ten days and you're barging in on her
uninvited in the middle of night.

TOM

She said we should come up anytime the living room lights are
on, which they clearly are.

CHARLIE

At least call first.

TOM

And wake up her parents?

CHARLIE

You act as if her apartment were your living room.

TOM

It is my living room.

INT. FOYER OUTSIDE FOWLER APARTMENT – NIGHT

*Charlie and Tom waiting at the door as Sally opens it. She is breathless
and disheveled, and there is a mysterious commotion behind her.*

SALLY

What are you doing here?

TOM

(*Defensively*) You said that we should come up if we saw your
lights on.

CHARLIE

Sorry to bother you.

An awkward moment. "The whole thing was a bit awkward."

SALLY

Actually, I was just about to go out.

TOM

Oh.

Who is it?

Sally feels she must invite them in and introduce them to her mystery guest now.

SALLY

(*To Allen:*) Just some friends. (*To them:*) Well, come on in.

They follow her into the Fowler apartment. Sitting on the library sofa drinking a cocktail is ALLEN TREEN, *a sleazy young-middle-aged man, dressed in expensive poor taste, who looks like he might be a record company executive.*

SALLY

Allen, these are my friends Charlie and Tommy. Allen is the record producer who discovered the Hated Few.

CHARLIE

They're very good.

ALLEN

Yes, they are. And Sally's going to be very good – she's got a lovely voice.

Charlie and Tom look at Sally.

I think we also have a friend in common – Rick Von Sloneker.

CHARLIE

You're a friend of Rick's?

ALLEN

Sure. Rick's a great guy – our houses are next to each other in Southampton –

SALLY

(*Breaking in*) Gosh, it's late. (*To Allen:*) We'd better be going. (*To them:*) Sorry, I don't think there's time for drinks after all.

EXT. AVENUE ADJACENT TO FOWLER BUILDING — NIGHT

Under the building awning Tom talks with Sally, with Charlie standing nearby, as the doorman tries to find a cab. At first Allen is at the curb, but he later rejoins them.

                        TOM
Do you have any idea when everyone's getting back? It's as if the whole SFRP had disintegrated.

                        SALLY
Vacation's almost over. We can't just keep getting together with the same people every night for the rest of our lives.

                        TOM
I don't see why not.

                        SALLY
It's inevitable that things get more back to normal sometime.

                        TOM
This wasn't normal?

                        SALLY
No.

                        TOM
I wish someone had told me that before. Do you know at least when Cynthia and Audrey are getting back?

                        SALLY
(*Exasperated*) I don't know. . . . That's their affair. . . .

                        ALLEN
(*Reminding Sally*) Your friend Cynthia's gone to that house party at Rick's.

                        TOM
In Southampton?

Allen nods.

                        SALLY
I'm not sure she was really going. . . . You guys are so tiresome.

265

A taxi swerves over to a stop near the awning; after perfunctory goodbyes Sally and Allen start heading for it.

EXT. AVENUE – NIGHT

Charlie and Tom walking down avenue.

> CHARLIE
>
> That was really embarrassing. Thanks for including me.

> TOM
>
> (*Stunned*) I can't believe it. God.

> CHARLIE
>
> Maybe underneath it all he's a nice guy. He doesn't make a very good first impression.

> TOM
>
> Not that – what he said about Cynthia. If Audrey's supposed to be visiting Cynthia in Connecticut, and Cynthia's with Von Sloneker in Southampton – what does that mean?

> CHARLIE
>
> That Audrey and Cynthia are in different states.

> TOM
>
> Are you trying to be thick? There's only one explanation – Audrey's gone with Cynthia to Von Sloneker's "house party" in Southampton!

> CHARLIE
>
> You're always selling Audrey awfully short, aren't you? I find that really despicable.

> TOM
>
> Could you stop calling me "despicable"? I'm worried about Audrey. Jane says that since that "Truth" session she's been in a very strange mood; she's said some really odd things. She told Jane she didn't feel like a "real woman."

> CHARLIE
>
> (*Surprised*) She said that?

TOM

It's the way Cynthia talks. . . .

INT. LIBRARY, BLACK APARTMENT – NIGHT

Tom is sitting in an armchair grasping its arms. Charlie stands.

CHARLIE

. . . I can't really share your concern – Audrey wouldn't put herself in the situation you describe. She has very clear views about these things – you know she's a big admirer of Jane Austen.

TOM

But she's turned her back on all that.

CHARLIE

I don't believe that. She's probably at home asleep right now, with the pink coverlet tucked in tight, and her stuffed animals looking over her.

TOM

Let's call her, then.

CHARLIE

We can't.

TOM

It's only a local call.

CHARLIE

We can't call her up now. It's nearly . . . (*looks at watch*) . . . three a.m. We'd wake her parents up

TOM

This is important for them, too. What if she's already at Von Sloneker's? I'm sure *he's* not asleep.

Charlie shakes head negatively.

If we told them why we were calling, they'd thank us.

INT. ELEVATOR LANDING, BLACK APARTMENT — NIGHT

Some time later. Tom with overcoat on but a bit askew; he's very drunk. Charlie showing him out.

CHARLIE

Older people tend to get up really early: I'll call the Rougets at seven. If there's any risk of Audrey's going to Von Sloneker's I'll call you right away. I don't expect to have to.

TOM

Could you call me either way?

CHARLIE

At seven?

Tom emphatically nods "yes."

Okay.

TOM

What if she's already at Von Sloneker's?

CHARLIE

Just relax – get some sleep.

Tom, drunk and trying to put rubber galoshes over his shoes, falls over and stays on the floor for a few moments.

Not here.

Tom gets up.

TOM

I've never been this drunk before. The problem is, with Fred no longer drinking, I can't pace myself.

CHARLIE

I'll call you.

TOM

Thanks. You're not such a bad fellow – though not too bright.

The elevator arrives and Tom gets in.

I don't mean that.

Tom blocks the elevator doors open.

                    CHARLIE
I'll call you.

                    TOM
Call me.

The elevator doors close on Tom.

INT. MAID'S ROOM, TOWNSEND APARTMENT — NIGHT

*The undrawn shade allows city light to illuminate the room. Tom sleeps
restlessly. He wakes up with a start and looks at a clock – it is 4:48. He
turns over and goes back to sleep.*

MONTAGE

*Tom's repeated waking up and nervously checking the clock alternates
with worrisome images of Audrey – reprises of earlier incidents which in
retrospect carry a disturbing import (times when he was unkind to her
in the past, conversations relating to Von Sloneker's cruel escapades)
and some Tom did not witness but which he imagines (her telling Jane,
"I hate him"). Also interspersed are imagined scenes of Audrey at Von
Sloneker's. Tom wakes up at 4:53, 4:59, 5:05, 5:07 – he perspires,
tosses and turns, and mumbles things in his sleep. Alcohol, romantic
worry and a guilty conscience have combined to ill effect.*

DAY FOURTEEN

INT. KITCHEN, TOWNSEND APARTMENT — DARK MORNING

*According to the clock, 7:05. The phone rings. Tom rushes out of his
room and grabs the receiver. The telephone conversation is heard from
Tom's side only.*

                    TOM
– Yes.
– What do you mean?!

269

    – Okay. Where?
    – Okay.
    – Goodbye.

Tom hangs up and hurries back to his room, a look of intense worry on his face.

EXT. MIDTOWN STREET – DAY

Charlie and Tom in galoshes trudge through slush.

> **CHARLIE**
> I called Audrey's parents at exactly seven – it turns out they're
> not such early risers. They thought Audrey was visiting
> Cynthia in Connecticut, too. So I called Cynthia's. Her
> mother answered – apparently she was sleeping late, too.
> (*Ominously.*) She said that Cynthia was visiting Audrey.

> **TOM**
> Jesus.

> **CHARLIE**
> Cynthia borrowed her mother's car. The last anyone had seen
> of either of them was about four yesterday afternoon.

> **TOM**
> (*Very worried*) So they might have already gotten to Von
> Sloneker's last night.

For a moment they say nothing.

> **CHARLIE**
> You were right.

Tom says nothing, just looks grim, as they continue walking and enter a Hertz Rent-a-Car office.

INT. HERTZ OFFICE – DAY

First, Charlie and Tom waiting in line, exchange concerned looks. It is apparent Tom is suffering from a hangover from the night before. Second, Charlie and Tom standing at counter while CLERK *looks at Charlie's MasterCard.*

CLERK

(*Looking at card*) Are you Gertrude Black?

CHARLIE

I'm authorized to use that card. I've often used it before.

EXT. ADJACENT SIDEWALK — DAY

Tom and Charlie walking disappointedly from Hertz office, Charlie particularly chagrined.

INT. INSIDE BANK DOORS — DAY

Charlie counting wad of cash with Tom looking on.

EXT. MIDTOWN STREET — DAY

Tom and Charlie walking through slush.

INT. AVIS OFFICE — DAY

A pretty and cheerful attendant completing form while Tom and Charlie wait at counter.

ATTENDANT

You do cash-qualify, sir.

CHARLIE

Good.

ATTENDANT

You will both be driving?

CHARLIE

No, he will be. (*Indicates Tom.*)

TOM

No, you'll be driving.

EXT. SIDEWALK ADJACENT TO OFFICE – DAY

Tom and Charlie leaving Avis office chagrined and humiliated.

CHARLIE

I can't believe you don't have a license.

TOM

Of course I don't – I live in Manhattan.

CHARLIE

I'm really surprised.

TOM

Oh, give me a break! I don't go out to the Hamptons. You could have gotten one easily.

CHARLIE

I'm no jock.

TOM

God, what a disaster!

CHARLIE

I'm going to get a license soon. This must be how the failure starts – an incompetence in mastering the common tasks of everyday life.

TOM

Doesn't Fred have a license?

INT. MANHATTAN COFFEE SHOP – DAY

Charlie finishing a call on a pay phone while Tom listens.

CHARLIE

Okay. Goodbye.

Charlie hangs up phone and turns back toward Tom.

CHARLIE

He says he can't, that he's about to get fired as it is.

TOM

He was always saying what a lousy job it was. . . . Did you tell him how serious the situation is?

CHARLIE

Yes.

TOM

He was always complaining about how lousy his job is.

CHARLIE

You know, it's possible that, to other people, the situation might not seem so ominous as it does to you and me. What can really happen? It's hard to believe that Audrey would get in such a situation as to need rescuing by us. . . .

Of course, you have been right up to now and Von Sloneker is a bad guy – capable of anything. It might sound melo-dramatic to say he's "ruined" girls – what does that really mean today – but it's true. He's done unspeakable things. And if Audrey's as upset and bitter as it seems, anything could happen. And what happens might not be entirely up to her. So she could be in a really dangerous situation – we've got to get out there as fast as possible.

TOM

And while we're here, flailing around, anything could be happening at Von Sloneker's. If only Nick were here – he'd know how to handle this.

CHARLIE

And he has all sorts of licenses and credit cards.

TOM

What would Nick do? How would he have gotten out of this?

They both think.

You have quite a bit of cash on you now?

CHARLIE

Yes. Lots.

273

EXT. STREET OUTSIDE COFFEE SHOP — DAY

Tom and Charlie flag Checker cab. When it stops Charlie talks with driver.

EXT. TRIBORO BRIDGE/LONG ISLAND EXPRESSWAY — DAY

The cab races by the outer boroughs. Tom and Charlie lean back in vinyl upholstery in somewhat intimidated silence. They are exhausted from the morning struggle, lack of sleep and apprehension about what might happen during the pending confrontation at Von Sloneker's. On the cab radio and the soundtrack the song "Volare" plays loudly. As the cab moves onto the Long Island Expressway, the passing scenery becomes less urban.

INT. CAB — DAY

Tom and Charlie.

> CHARLIE
> Whenever I think we might be overreacting, I think about Polly Perkins.

> TOM
> Or Cathy Livingstone.

> CHARLIE
> I think I knew her.

EXT. LONG ISLAND EXPRESSWAY — DAY

Passing scenery.

INT. CAB — DAY

Tom and Charlie.

> CHARLIE
> What are you going to do when we get there?

> TOM
> I don't know. It depends what the situation is.

274

Tom looks with preoccupied air at passing scenery.

INT. CAB – DAY

Tom and Charlie.

> TOM
>
> Yesterday I was thinking. Maybe Fourier was a crank – his ideas completely unworkable.

> CHARLIE
>
> Well, I wouldn't want to live on a farm.

INT. CAB – DAY

Tom and Charlie.

> CHARLIE
>
> You know Rick's a really big guy. He might not be too pleased to see us.

> TOM
>
> I've thought of that.

The car approaches the South Fork of Suffolk County. A sign indicates Southampton. Montage of desolate Southampton of late December: deserted beach club, other clubs and summer haunts. The car passes through town to Gin Lane and turns into driveway of Von Sloneker's house (actually his mother's). Tom, Charlie and the driver get out of the cab.

> CHARLIE
>
> (*To driver:*) Thanks a lot. We shouldn't be long.

> DRIVER
>
> Take as long as you want. I'm going now.

> CHARLIE
>
> We need you to take us back. That was understood.

> DRIVER
>
> No one said this was a two-way. You think I'm going to wait around here New Year's Eve, you're crazy.

275

Cut image before sound, to follow Tom while dialog continues.

EXT. HOUSE — DAY

Tom warily examines the house's exterior, listening for any commotion inside, and pondering how he should enter.

[O.s. dispute between Charlie and the driver can still be heard.

CHARLIE

I'm sorry for this misunderstanding.

DRIVER

That's all right – my money?

CHARLIE

I don't know how we're going to get back.

DRIVER

What's this shit?

CHARLIE

A gratuity is included.

DRIVER

What's this shit?]

EXT. ALONGSIDE CAB — DAY.

Charlie's dispute with the driver is still in progress.

CHARLIE

But you're not taking us back.

DRIVER

That doesn't matter – you gotta pay for my time.

CHARLIE

But we want to go back with you.

DRIVER

I'm sick of taking lip from young snots like you, pretending to be high rollers without the funds.

Charlie, after a long pause, takes a check from his wallet.

CHARLIE

I only have 240 in cash – I'll have to give you a check for the rest.

DRIVER

I don't take checks.

EXT. VON SLONEKER DRIVEWAY – DAY

Tom, returning from the house, approaches Charlie while the cab backs up, turns around and then guns out of the driveway, sending gravel flying.

CHARLIE

I was sure we had agreed on 120 as the full price.

EXT. HOUSEFRONT – DAY

Other side of silent, ostensibly empty house, is shown. Tom and Charlie enter the frame cautiously walking down path. Charlie stops and leans down to pick up something lying alongside the path – a piece of colorful fabric of some kind.

CHARLIE

Look at this.

TOM

What is it?

CHARLIE

It looks like some girl's panties.

TOM

Oh Jesus. That bastard.

INT. VON SLONEKER HOUSE – DAY

Tom hurries to the door and pushes it open, with Charlie following. Loud music – a rock song featuring disgusting grunts and subhuman lyrics – "uhn, uhn, oh baby, oh baby, gimme your lovin', oh baby, oh baby," etc. – comes from the second floor. Tom runs up the stairway and along the corridor, noting the disposition of the rooms, until

reaching the closed double-doors from behind which the music comes.
Tom tries the doors, which seem to be locked; he prepares to lunge
against them as Charlie reaches him. Tom pushes against the doors
with his shoulder; with Charlie he pushes a second time. This time the
door opens abruptly – opened by Victor Lemley, who wears only a
bathing suit and a layer of suntan oil. Tom and Charlie are temporarily
blinded by an extremely powerful light. The tableau in front of them is
not reassuring: Cynthia and Audrey, wearing only bikinis (in
Cynthia's case unhooked), lie on towels spread over the carpet, their
skin greased with suntan oil; above, a sunlamp rigged up for tanning
purposes. A greasy-skinned semi-nude Von Sloneker, Audrey and
Cynthia, and an unknown sunbathing guy and girl look startled by
their arrival. Tom and Charlie are also silenced by the strange scene.

VON SLONEKER

What are you clowns doing here?!

TOM

What are you doing?

VON SLONEKER

This is my place – I can do whatever I want here.

TOM

That's not true.

VON SLONEKER

Oh, no?

TOM

You couldn't formulate a coherent sentence here.

VON SLONEKER

How dare you break in here – (*To Lemley, indicating doorknob:*)
Did they break that?

CYNTHIA

(*To Charlie and Tom:*) What are you doing here? – This is really
embarrassing.

CHARLIE

A little embarrassment could do you some good. . . . (*To Von*
Sloneker:) By the way (*holding up panties*), whose are these?

278

VON SLONEKER

(*Snatches and examines them in tasteless manner*) I haven't the slightest idea. Now get out of here, twerps.

AUDREY

They buy the panties new and scatter them around. It's one of Rick's little delicacies.

VON SLONEKER

That's a lie. (*To intruders:*) Take this flat-chested, goody-goody, pain-in-the-neck with you as you go.

TOM

She's not a goody-goody.

VON SLONEKER

Before you go . . .

Von Sloneker rabbit-punches Tom in the stomach. As Tom doubles over in pain and surprise, Victor Lemley grabs him from behind so that his upper arms are pinned. The third guy grabs Charlie the same way. Tom's hands and forearms remain free and he slips a small silvery object from his left jacket pocket. Von Sloneker, aproaching to continue the beating, sees the object in Tom's hand and freezes.

Jeezus – he's got a gun.

He, Lemley and the other guy all back off. There is a moment of stunned silence.

CYNTHIA

(*To Tom:*) Are you crazy?

Tom nods affirmatively – he's still partly hunched over from Von Sloneker's punch and too winded to speak.

CHARLIE

I warn you, he's a Fourierist.

LEMLEY

(*To Rick:*) That gun's a joke, Rick. It's a toy or antique or something.

VON SLONEKER

Yeah . . . well . . . let the jerk play his little game.

279

EXT. SOUTHAMPTON BEACH – LATE AFTERNOON/SUNSET

Tom and Audrey stand near each other on the beach as if they were talking. In the background, up from the beach, Charlie talks into a pay phone.

TOM

Did anything happen?

AUDREY

Of course not.

TOM

You mean you were never interested in Von Sloneker at all?

Audrey silent for a long while, teasingly implying ambivalence, but then an expression indicating "of course not, you fool."

Then why did you come out?

AUDREY

To get a suntan. . . . And the whole thing with the Rat Pack was getting claustrophobic. And Cynthia insisted I come – she's terribly impressed with Rick.

TOM

It's not something Jane Austen would have done.

AUDREY

No. (*Pause.*) I suppose Europe is over there. (*She points directly over the ocean.*)

TOM

No. That would be Brazil. Europe is more that way. (*Points eastward, parallel to beach.*) You're really going back next week?

AUDREY

I think so.

TOM

What can you study in France that you can't study here?

AUDREY

French. Actually, I was thinking of coming back when this semester ends.

TOM

I was thinking of going over – not necessarily to Grenoble, but to France and Italy – though my resources are limited.

AUDREY

There are some awfully cheap air fares these days – it seems a shame not to take advantage of them.

TOM

That's how I feel.

A pause.

AUDREY

Do you really think I'm flat-chested?

TOM

I haven't really thought about it. . . . Well, I shouldn't say that. The thing is, you look great – and that's what's important. You don't want to overdo it.

In the background Charlie has finished his telephone calls and is walking toward them. They walk up toward him.

A WINTRY "GIN LANE" OR NEARBY ROAD

Tom, Charlie and Audrey walking along, hitchhiking, with cars passing. We see them from the perspective of an approaching Jaguar or Mercedes, driven by a man dressed in evening clothes for New Year's Eve. He briefly slows down but finally does not stop. They look up. After passing the man looks at them in his mirror; we see them diminishing in size in the distance. The camera stays with the man in the car, and returns to the perspective of the road ahead.